Royal
Indian Recipes

Royal
Indian Recipes

Compiled by the Master Chefs of
THE ASHOK GROUP OF HOTELS

Photographs
Deepak Budhraja

Food styling
Preeti Budhraja

Lustre Press
·
Roli Books

First published by
Lustre Press Pvt. Ltd.
M-75 GK II Market, New Delhi-110048, INDIA
Phones: (011) 644 2271/646 2782/0886/0887
Fax: (011) 646 7185

Reprinted in 1999

© **Lustre Press Pvt. Ltd. 1997**
© **Recipes, India Tourism Development Corporation**

ISBN: 81-7437-077-3

Photographer
Deepak Budhraja

Food styling
Preeti Budhraja

Production
N.K. Nigam, Abhijit Raha

Design
Sarita Verma Mathur

Project co-ordinator
Lavinia Rao

Typesetting
Naresh L. Mondal

Printed and bound by
APP Printing, Singapore

Acknowledgment

We are grateful for the guidance and cooperation of officers
and staff of the Publicity & Production Division of the
India Tourism Development Corporation, New Delhi
The Ashok Hotel, New Delhi and
Hyderabad House, New Delhi.
Our special thanks to
Mr. Anil Bhandari, Mr. Saleem Hamid, Ms. Chandni Luthra,
Mr. Mahesh Kapoor, Mr. Narendra Piplani
and the Master Chefs
Jaganmoy Chaudhury and Sudhir Sibbal.

**This book is dedicated to all the Master Chefs,
past and present, of the Ashok Group of Hotels, India**

CONTENTS

Introduction

*T*hrough a unique repertoire of traditional favourites and classic standbys of the timeless Indian cuisine, the Master Chefs of India have for centuries endeavoured to woo the palate of visiting foreign dignitaries. Foremost amongst these culinary craftsmen are the Master Chefs of the Ashok Group of Hotels.

The Ashok Chefs have for long been held in high esteem the world over for their super cuisine. Their consummate skills, backed by high standards of service which have been evolved for hosting important State Banquets have endeared them to various Heads of States. A selection of some of the choicest recipes from these numerous occasions are given in this book, which opens a window on the culinary secrets of these Master Chefs.

The State Banquet is a prestigious means of honouring India's VIP guests. The fabled Indian hospitality tradition gives the *atithi* or the guest a place of high honour. In addition, the pomp and ceremony, which is so much a part of our cultural heritage, makes these regal banquets an unforgettable experience. With the skilful contributions of the Ashok Master Chefs, these intrinsically Indian celebrations have been enriched with additional splendour.

The impeccable arrangements for such prestigious events have been over the years, fine-tuned to a ceremonial statement of graciousness and elegance, with a dazzling co-ordination of Indian skills and services. Prime Minister Indira Gandhi's inaugural banquet for 103 VVIPS attending the Non-Aligned Movement Conference at the Ashok in the early 80s was the perfect consummation of Indian hospitality.

Catering for State Banquets is no easy task. It requires special skills and dexterous co-ordination to provide that seamless core to the protocol and ceremonial ambience that such an important event demands. Attention to detail is the invisible thread that holds the entire ceremony together. The focal point of a banquet is not only the food, but every aspect that makes up a superb table. This includes, the choice of invitees, the venue, the beauty of the table setting, the decor, the service, the entertainment . . . the stamp of a ceremonial formality that raises the entire proceeding to a regal plane. Special training and innovativeness comprise the backbone of the Ashok's meticulous contributions to match the dignity and elegance of the ceremony befitting its frequent and august assemblage of guests.

Among the more popular venues for such grand banquets, hosted by the President, the Vice-President, the Prime Minister and the Ministry of External Affairs, in New Delhi, are the Rashtrapati Bhawan, Hyderabad House and the Ashok Hotel. Hyderabad House, the erstwhile palace of the Nizam of Hyderabad, still preserves its regal 'olde worlde' ambience with its exquisite Persian and Kashmiri carpets, opulent chandeliers and period furniture.

The ceremonial proceedings require many days of careful planning. The hosts decide whether they need a long banquet table or smaller round ones to seat the 60-70 guests who will be attending the event. Elegance and harmony are the key notes for the aesthetic blending of flowers, crystal, china, cutlery and drapery. Though round tables (seven of them—with the Prime Minister and his chief guests being placed at the central one) have replaced the rectangular table at Hyderabad House they do not detract from the formality of the occasion. Table placement and the choice of guests can be a highly touchy affair. Things can become pretty dicey if Kings and Presidents and Prime Ministers have to share the limelight . . .

Dressed in black *bandhgallas* with gold braiding and in white in summers, specially trained, liveried attendants are positioned behind the embossed chairs in the banquet hall. The service itself is a highly fine-tuned affair and must be in keeping with the importance and formality of the occasion and the need to flawlessly serve all the guests simultaneously. Specialised training is imparted to the stewards who are involved in the serving and clearing of the meal. The entire process is highly regimented.

Two tentative menus are sent by the Ashok Chefs to the hosts for approval, well in advance. In this time, any changes, testing and tasting of meals (also for security reasons) can be conducted with ease. The menu itself generally consists of an *entree*, a soup, chicken and lamb, vegetables, rice, *naans*, *papad*, dessert, fruit and coffee.

In the earlier days there was a greater component of continental fare on the menus. Later, Indian Prime Ministers, including Indira Gandhi and Rajiv Gandhi, introduced a larger variety of Indian culinary delights for their guests. One of the Master Chefs recalls Indira Gandhi's keenness to introduce Indian dishes at banquets, even though she personally enjoyed continental fare immensely. Her interest in menu planning played an inspiring role in the chefs own innovativeness. However, her desire to introduce some Indian innovation in a Western meal sometimes tested the culinary skills of the chefs. Chef Sibbal recounts how at one of her banquets 'roast turkey with chestnut sauce' was served with *biryani*! Initially it caused much consternation but eventually the combination turned out to be such a great success with her foreign guests, that it was often repeated at subsequent banquets. On another occasion Prime Minister Rajiv Gandhi suggested that 'chicken liverpate' be served with baby *naans*, instead of the   traditional bread. Needless to say, it was a great hit!

It was during Rajiv Gandhi's tenure as Prime Minister that   Nouvelle Cuisine came into its own at the State Banquets. And though he insisted that the chefs cut down on oil, he encouraged them to be more inventive and original. A great deal of research and experimentation resulted in some astonishingly exotic dishes.

With former Prime Minister Narasimha Rao and former President R. Venkataraman, banquets saw the increase of south dishes on the menu. While Narasimha enjoyed his 'Gangura pickle-stuffed *idlis*', his guests   Indian Rao tried baby *uttapams*, baby *dosas*, baby *idlis*.

The 'tandoori' platter enjoys unrivalled popularity as an *entree* dish at the banguets. The succulent *tikkas* and melting *kababs* have seduced the tastebuds of foreign guests with repeated success. Hillary Clinton is known to have succumbed to the 'chicken *lehsuniya tikkas*', while guests at President Zakir Hussain's table were assured of excellent 'mughlai' delights. An ex-foriegn secretary recalls, with a nostalgic gleam in his eyes, how for every new *kabab* offered to non-vegetarian guests, there would be an equivalent vegetarian option for those who did not eat meat.

Catering to the personal preference of a guest is in itself a feat. For example, when the Secretary of State Henry Kissinger was scheduled to visit India, it was learned that he was very fond of rhododendron juice. Now this is not available in any grocery store in Delhi. A bit of research revealed that it was in fact a speciality of Himachal Pradesh. A carton of this juice was flown in from Shimla and served to him on his arrival. He was reported to have been most touched by the gesture.

While checking out the likes and dislikes of Hillary Clinton, America's First Lady, it was learnt that she and President Bill Clinton were regulars at an Indian restaurant in Washington, New York, where she particularly enjoyed the 'Mangalorean prawn curry in cococnut *masala*'. Imagine her pleasure when it was served to her at a personal luncheon at Race Course Road, the house of the Prime Minister. During the NAM banqueting days, one of the VIP Arab guests enjoyed the *naans* so much that he ordered 40 of them for breakfast! The Saudi Prince was so entranced by our fragrant basmati rice he even took some home. Begum Yakub Khan enjoyed the freshly ground south indian coffee to such a degree that she felt compelled to see how it was prepared. Shimon Peres, the then Foreign Secretary of Israel, was only served *kosher* food on his visit. While the Aga Khan disliked garlic and avoided prawns, Zambia's Kenneth Kaunda relished the *dosas* and *idlis*.

The use of spices at an Indian State Banquet needs to be monitored to suit the visitors' tastes. Even though many visitors during NAM, such as the Guyanan President, had a predeliction for red hot chillies, others preferred to temper its flavour. Indira Gandhi herself was very particular about the quality and the quantity of spices used in the food. She would even check on the amount of *methi* used to ensure that it did not aggravate the throat of her guests. In fact, she often suggested that they acquire purer homemade spices from some women's charity organisation which may have been on her list of support at that time.

Indira Gandhi also introduced pomegranate juice and grape juice instead of the regular *mausambi* and orange juice one invariably found during cocktails. Narasimha Rao had a penchant for *jal jeera*. Since no liquor is served at an Indian State banquet (not even liqueur chocolate) even the toasts to quests are made with apple juice or some such alternative.

Personalised entertainment of State guests have been arranged at Race Course Road by Rajiv Gandhi and Narasimha Rao, lending an air of informality and the opportunity to experiment with much spicier and exotic fare for the smaller table. Hillary Clinton was treated to a very elaborate north Indian meal, which included an excellent selection of fish and 'tandoori' delicacies, served on a *thali*. When Indira Gandhi organized any such meal she would consult closely with her chef to ensure that the meal was perfectly cooked and included a variety of dishes to enhance her table. Keenly aware of ensuring the comfort of her guests, she once threw an informal meal for Prince Charles at the Rashtrapati Bhawan lawns, where she invited people of his own age group, to counteract the formal banquet given earlier.

'I don't want a dumb table' she once told an ex-foreign secretary, as she went through the guest list and discussed how they would be seated. This was her way of ensuring that the conversation at the banquet was lively and compatible, even though the banquet was a formal affair. Highly conscious of what was happening . . . even down to the last few guests seated at the end of the table, she would urge, in a very discreet manner of course, people to participate in the flow of conversation. Another invitee recalls her consternation when despite her urgings, the women invitees were too much in awe of Queen Elizabeth, resplendent in a gorgeous gown and her twinkling tiara, to muster up enough small chat at the Ashok Hall during the pre-dinner gathering.

Presentation of food itself acts as an excellent appetiser. No one knew this better than Indira Gandhi, who was an excellent and fastidious hostess. Her own aesthetic sense was particularly heightened, and her displeasure was highly noticeable if things were not exactly right. On one occasion she had given instructions that scissors must be placed with the grape bunches when the fruit was brought in. To her observant eye, the chain reaction of her guests plucking the grapes with their hands caused her more than little agitation. Summoning one of the attendants discreetly she inquired why the scissors were missing. The flustered man pointed out that the scissors were indeed placed with the grapes as she had instructed . . . but no one was using them. The ceremonial aspect of the banquet is augmented by the strict protocol maintained from the moment the guests enter the gracious environs of Hyderabad House. The guests are presented to the visiting Heads of State, invited to eat the elaborate meal. They leave the banquet only after they are personally seen off by the Prime Minister.

It is this strict protocol and formality which adds a strong element of elegance and regality to the entire progress of the banquet. As the lights dim . . . after the beautifully orchestrated ceremony . . . an aura of muted fanfare lingers long after the guests have gone . . . Echoing the flavour of unforgettable evenings amidst gracious splendour, accompanied by culinary delights and wonderous company, is the selection of recipes from the Master Chefs of the Ashok Group to experiment with and savour.

—Ranee Sahaney

9

Raee (Mustard) Seeds

Tej Patta (Bay Leaves)

Star Anise

Choti Elaichi (Green Cardamom)

Kalonji (Onion) Seeds

Sonth (Dry Ginger)

Saunf (Fennel) Seeds

Javitri (Mace)

Bari Elaichi (Black Cardamom)

Methi Dana (Fenugreek Seeds)

Kali Mirch (Black Pepper Corns)

Red Chillies, whole

Daalchini (Cinnamon)

Ajwain (Carom) Seeds

Dhania (Coriander) Seeds

Zeera (Cumin) Seeds

Laung (Cloves)

Jaiphal (Nutmeg)

Khus Khus
(Poppy
seeds)

Kala Namak
(Black Rock Salt)

Sonth (Dry
Ginger)
Powder

al Mirch
Red Chilli)
owder

Chaat
Masala

Sambhar Powder

soori Methi (Dry
nugreek) Powder

White Pepper
Powder

Amchoor
(Dry
Mango)
Powder

Dhania (Coriander)
Powder

Haldi
(Turmeric)
Powder

Zeera (Cumin) Powder

Heeng (Asafoetida)
Powder

Namak
(Salt)

Garam Masala

Til (Sesame)
Seeds

Garam
Masala

Onions,
browned

Garlic Paste

Ginger
Paste

Khoya

Cottage Cheese
(Paneer)

Onion
Paste

Tomato
Purée

Basic Indian Recipes

Ginger Paste:
Soak ginger (250 gms) overnight to soften the skin. Peel and chop roughly. Process until pulped, using very little water if required. The plup can be stored in an air tight container and refrigerated for 4-6 weeks

Garlic Paste:
Soak garlic (250 gms) overnight to soften the skin. Peel the garlic cloves and chop roughly. Process until pulped, using very little water if required. The pulp can be stored in an air tight container and refrigerated for 4-6 weeks.

Onion Paste:
Peel and chop the onions (500 gms) into quarters. Process until pulped, using very little water if required. The pulp can be stored in an air tight container and refrigerated for 4-6 weeks.

Brown Onion Paste:
Slice the onions (500 gms) and fry over medium heat until brown. Remove, drain excess oil and allow to cool. Process until pulped, using very little water if required. The pulp can be stored in an air tight container and refrigerated for 4-6 weeks.

Paneer (cottage cheese):
In a pot, put milk (3 litres) to boil. Just before it boils add lemon juice or white vinegar (60 ml / 4 tbs) to curdle the milk. Strain the curdled milk through a muslin cloth to allow all whey and moisture to drain. Allow to hang under a weight for 2-3 hours to set in a block which can be cut or grated.

Khoya:
Boil full cream milk (2 litres) in a kadhai (wok), reduce heat to low and boil till the milk is reduced to half, stirring occassionally. Continue cooking, now, stirring constantly and scrapping from the sides till a thick paste-like consistency is obtained (1-1 1/2 hours). Allow to cool and refrigerate. Use as required.

Onions, browned:
Peel and slice 2 large onions. Heat oil in a kadhai (wok) and fry the sliced onions on medium heat until golden brown. Remove and drain excess oil. Use immediately for garnishing any dish.

Tomato Purée:
Peel and chop the tomatoes (1 kg), remove the seeds. In a pan, cook the tomatoes on medium heat alongwith Water (1 litre), Cloves 8, Green cardamoms 8, Ginger 15 gms, Garlic 10 gms, Bayleaves 5 and Black peppercorns 5 gms, until the tomatoes are tender. Remove from heat, allow to cool and process until pulped. Can be stored in an air tight container and refrigerated for 4-6 weeks.

Garam Masala:
450 gms, broil the following ingredients in a thick bottomed pan. Cumin seeds (200 gms), Black pepper corns (35 gms), Black cardamom seeds (45 gms), Green cardamom (30 gms), Coriander seeds (60 gms), Cloves (20 gms), Cinnamom sticks (20 gms), Mace powder (20 gms), Bayleaves (15 gms), Ginger powder (30 gms), Nutmeg (2). Allow to cool and grind to a powder. Store in an air tight container and use as required.

SOUPS & JUICES

Clockwise from left: Tomato and Coconut Soup, Palak Shorba and Carrot and Orange Soup (page 19). Dahi Shorba, Tomato and Coriander Soup (page 17). Watermelon Juice, Bel ka Sharbat and Tender Coconut Shikanji (page 21), Haleem Shorba (page 23).

Cold Cucumber Soup

Green Cucumber blended with cream, served chilled

Serves: 4, Preparation time: 30 minutes, Cooking time: 45 minutes

Ingredients:

Cucumber, quartered alongwith peel .... *1 kg*	Salt to taste
Butter .... *25 gms / 5 tsp*	White pepper powder .... *3 gms / ½ tsp*
Onions, quartered .... *200 gms / 1 cup*	Cream, whipped .... *100 gms / ½ cup*
Vegetable stock, strained .... *2 litres / 10 cups*	

Method:

1. Heat butter in a pot, add onions and sauté till transparent, add the cucumber and sauté for a few minutes.
2. Stir in the veg.stock, salt to taste and white pepper powder. Cover and cook on low heat for 20-25 minutes till the cucumber is cooked and tender. Stir in the cream, remove from heat and allow to cool.
3. Blend the soup to obtain a purée and strain through a muslin cloth.
4. Transfer to a soup bowl and refrigerate for 1 hour.
5. Serve chilled, garnished with cream. (Picture on page 15).

Dahi Shorba

Tangy yoghurt soup

Serves: 4, Preparation time: 15 minutes, Cooking time: 25 minutes

Ingredients:

Yoghurt .... *300 gms / 1½ cups*	Turmeric *(haldi)* powder .... *5 gms / 1 tsp*
Butter .... *25 gms / 5 tbs*	White Radish, peeled, cut into cubes .... *225 gms / 1 cup*
Fenugreek *(methi)* seeds .... *10 gms / 2 tsp*	Water .... *3 lt / 15 cups*
Mustard *(raee)* seeds .... *10 gms / 2 tsp*	Curry leaves .... *10 gms / 2 tsp*
Gramflour *(besan)* .... *150 gms / ¾ cup*	Curry powder .... *5 gms / 1 tsp*
Salt to taste	Cream .... *100 gms/ ½ cup*
White pepper powder .... *5 gms / 1 tsp*	

Method:

1. Melt butter in a pot, add fenugreek and mustard seeds, sauté till they crackle, add gramflour, salt, white pepper powder, turmeric powder, and radish blended in yoghurt.
2. Add water (1 litre / 5 cups) and cook till a pleasing smell of gramflour emanates. Reduce heat and simmer for 10 minutes.
3. Add the remaining water and curry leaves, cook on low heat till it comes to a boil. Stir in the curry powder.
4. Remove from heat and pass through a soup strainer.
5. Stir in the cream, transfer to soup bowls and serve.

Tomato and Coriander Soup

Cream of tomato braised with coriander

Serves: 4, Preparation time: 15 minutes, Cooking time: 35 minutes

Ingredients:

Tomatoes, chopped .... *500 gms / 2½ cups*	Bayleaves *(tej patta)* 4
Butter .... *30 gms / 2 tbs*	Salt .... *15 gms / 1 tbs*
Coriander seeds .... *2 gms / ⅓ tsp*	White pepper powder .... *3 gms / ½ tsp*
Ginger, chopped .... *5 gms / 1 tsp*	Vegetable stock .... *1½ litre / 7 cups*
Garlic, chopped .... *5 gms / 1 tsp*	Orange/Red colour .... *5 gms / 1 tsp*
Flour .... *40 gms / 2 ⅔ tbs*	Green coriander, chopped .... *20 gms / 4 tsp*

Method:

1. Melt butter in a handi *(pot)*, add coriander seeds and sauté till they crackle. Add ginger and garlic and sauté for a minute.
2. Add flour and cook to a sandy texture without colouring, add the tomatoes and sauté for a few minutes.
3. Stir in the remaining ingredients except green coriander and cook for about 20 minutes.
4. Remove from heat and pass through a soup strainer.
5. Add the green coriander and reheat till it comes to a boil.
6. Remove from heat and transfer to soup bowls.
7. Serve immediately, garnished with green coriander.

Tomato and Coconut Soup

Tomato soup laced with coconut milk

Serves: 4, Preparation time: 15 minutes, Cooking time: 30 minutes

Ingredients:

Tomatoes,chopped .... 500 gms / 2 ½ cups	Salt to taste
Coconut, grated...................................... 100 gms / ½ cup	White pepper powder .... 2 gms / ⅓ tsp
Coconut oil .... 40 ml / 2 ⅔ tbs	Bayleaves *(tej patta)* 4
Garlic, chopped.. 10 gms / 2 tsp	Vegetable stock .... 1 ½ litres / 7 cups
Onions, chopped .... 50 gms / 3 ⅓ tbs	Cream.. 40 gms / 2 ⅔ tbs
Ginger, crushed....................................... 15 gms / 1 tbs	

Method:

1. Heat coconut oil in a pot. Sauté garlic and onions for a few seconds.
2. Add coconut and stir-fry. Add tomatoes and ginger.
3. Stir in the salt, white pepper powder, bayleaves and vegetable stock. Allow to simmer for 15-20 minutes till the tomatoes are cooked and tender.

4. Remove from heat and allow to cool.
5. Blend to obtain a purée, strain through a muslin cloth and reheat.
6. Remove from heat and stir in the cream.
7. Transfer to soup bowl and serve immediately.

Palak Shorba

Cumin and garlic flavoured veloute of spinach

Serves: 4, Preparation time: 20 minutes, Cooking time: 30 minutes

Ingredients:

Spinach *(palak)* .... 500 gms / 2 ½ cups	Black peppercorns .... 2 gms / ⅓ tsp
Butter .... 30 gms / 2 tbs	Bayleaves *(tej patta)* 4
Flour... 30 gms / 2 tbs	Salt to taste
Ginger, chopped .... 25 gms / 5 tsp	White pepper powder .... a pinch
Garlic, chopped.. 5 gms / 1 tsp	Vegetable stock .... 1 ½ litres / 7 cups

Method:

1. Chop the spinach leaves into small pieces and wash thoroughly.
2. Melt buttter in a handi *(pot)*. Add flour and cook to a sandy texture.
3. Add ginger, garlic, spinach and sauté for a few minutes. Add black peppercorns and bayleaves.
4. Stir in the salt, white pepper powder and vegetable

stock. Simmer for 15-20 minutes.
5. Remove the spinach from the stock and blend to a purée. Return the spinach purée to the stock and cook for 5 minutes.
6. Remove from heat, transfer to soup bowls and serve hot.

Carrot and Orange Soup

Puréed carrots blended with orange juice, served hot

Serves: 4, Preparation time: 1 hour, Cooking time: 40 minutes

Ingredients:

Carrots, cut into small cubes .... 500 gms / 2 ½ cups	White pepper powder .... 2 gms / ⅓ tsp
Orange juice .... 800 ml / 4 cups	Sugar .... 50 gms / 3 ⅓ tbs
Butter .... 25 gms / 5 tsp	Cream... 100 gms / ½ cup
Onions, chopped .... 150 gms / ⅔ cup	
Salt to taste	

Method:

1. Heat butter in a pan, add the onion and sauté till transparent.
2. Add the carrots and sauté for a minute. Add the remaining ingredients except cream and cook on low heat till the carrot pieces are tender.

3. Remove and pass through a soup strainer and then strain through a muslin cloth.
4. Reheat the strained soup and stir in the cream.
5. Remove from heat and transfer to soup bowls.
6. Serve hot.

Watermelon Juice

A delightful blend of watermelon with a touch of mint

Serves: 4, Preparation time: 30 minutes

Ingredients:

Watermelons... *4.5 kgs*
Mint leaves, chopped.................................. *5 gms / 1 tsp*

Black rock salt *(kala namak)* to taste

Method:

1. Cut the flesh into small chunks and discard the rind.
2. Remove all the seeds, put in a mixie bowl with mint leaves.
3. Blend to make a purée.

4. Pass through a muslin cloth, discard the waste.
5. Chill in a refrigerator.
6. Pour into glasses and serve.

Bel ka Sharbat

Wood Apple Squash, a summer time favourite of all.

4 portions, Preparation time: 8-10 hours

Ingredients:

Bel *(large)* *1*
Water....................................... *1 litre / 5 cups*

Sugar, powdered .... *100 gms / ½ cup*

Method:

1. Break open the bel and remove the pulp.
2. Soak the pulp in water and leave to rest overnight.
3. Dissolve sugar in the bel water and strain through a

muslin cloth.
4. Chill in a refrigerator.
5. Pour into serving glass and serve.

Tender Coconut Shikanji

Ginger blended coconut water with a touch of lemon

Serves:4, Preparation time: 30 minutes.

Ingredients:

Green or Tender coconuts *4*
Sugar, powdered .... *150 gms / ¾ cup*

Lemon *3*
Ginger juice, strained .... *10 ml / 2 tsp*

Method:

1. Extract the water from the coconuts.
2. Dissolve sugar in the coconut water. Add juice of 3 lemons and ginger. Strain through a muslin cloth.

3. Chill in a refrigerator.
4. Pour to serving glasses and serve.

Broccoli and Walnut Soup

Creamed broccoli served with walnuts

Serves: 4, Preparation time: 15 minutes, Cooking time: 40 minutes

Ingredients:

Broccoli, florets only .... *400 gms / 2 cups*
Walnuts, chopped .... *16 gms / 1 tbs*
Butter .... *30 gms / 2 tbs*
Onions, chopped .... *30 gms / 2 tbs*
Garlic, chopped.. *5 gms / 1 tsp*
Leeks, chopped .... *20 gms / 4 tsp*

Celery, chopped .... *20 gms / 4 tsp*
Salt to taste
White pepper powder .... *2 gms / ⅓ tsp*
Vegetable stock .... *1 ½ litres / 7 cups*
Cream.. *100 gms / ½ cup*

Method:

1. Heat butter in a handi *(pot)*. Add onions and garlic, sauté for a minute. Add leeks, celery, broccoli, and stir-fry.
2. Stir in salt, white pepper powder and veg. stock. Simmer for 20 minutes until the broccoli is tender.
3. Remove the broccoli from the soup, allow to cool and

blend to a purée. Mix the purée into the soup, strain through a muslin cloth.
4. Reheat the strained soup and stir in the cream.
5. Remove from heat, transfer to soup bowls and serve hot, garnished with walnuts.

Rasam

Spicy and tangy lentil soup

Serves:4, Preparation time: 30-40 minutes, Cooking time:40 minutes.

Ingredients:

Lentils *(arhar daal)* .... 100 gms / ½ cup	Ginger, chopped .... 13 gms / 2 ⅓ tsp
Tamarind *(imli)* .... 40 gms / 2 ⅔ tsp	Black peppercorns .... 6 gms / 1 tsp
Turmeric *(haldi)* powder .... 6 gms / 1 tsp	Asafoetida *(heeng)* .... 3 gms / ½ tsp
Red chilli powder .... 8 gms / 1 ½ tsp	Water .... 1 litre / 5 cups
Salt .... 16 gms / 1tbs	**For the tempering:**
Coriander powder .... 16 gms / 1 tbs	Red chillies, whole .... 3 gms / ½ tsp
Tomatoes, quartered .... 160 gms / ¾ cup	Mustard *(raee)* seeds .... 8 gms / 1 ½ tsp
Cumin *(jeera)* seeds, powdered.............. 8 gms / 1 ½ tsp	Sesame *(til)* seeds .... 5 gms / 1 tsp
Garlic, chopped .... 8 gms / 1 ½ tsp	Curry leaves .... 1 sprig

Method:

1. Soak tamarind in water, squeeze out the pulp and discard waste.

2. Soak lentils in water for ½ hour. Drain and keep aside.

3. Heat the tamarind extract in a handi *(pot)*, add turmeric powder, red chilli powder, salt, coriander powder and tomatoes and cook on low heat for 20 minutes.

4. Add cumin, garlic, ginger, black peppercorns and asafoetida, mix well and cook for another 10 minutes.

5. Stir in the lentils alongwith water. Bring to a boil, reduce heat and cook for 10 minutes. Remove from heat and pass through a soup strainer.

6. For the tempering, heat oil in a pan, add red chillies, mustard seeds, sesame seeds and curry leaves. Sauté till they crackle.

7. Remove from heat and add this to the prepared soup.

8. Serve hot, as a starter or as an accompaniment to a meal.

Salted Lassi

Salted butter milk

Serves: 4, Preparation time: 15 minutes.

Ingredients:

Yoghurt .... 1 kg	Salt .... 15 gms / 1 tbs
Water .... 400 ml / 2 cups	Ice cubes .... 200 gms / 1 cup

Method:

1. Mix yoghurt alongwith water, salt and ice cubes until thoroughly mixed.

2. Pour into serving glasses.

3. Serve cold, as a starter or an accompaniment to a meal.

Haleem Shorba

Lamb broth laced with wheat milk

Serves: 4, Preparation time: 12-14 hours, Cooking time: 5 hours

Ingredients:

Lamb, bones .... 1 kg	White butter .... 50 gms / 3 ⅓ tbs
Wheat .... 100 gms / ½ cup	Onions, chopped .... 50 gms / 3 ⅓ tbs
Water .... 2 litres / 10 cups	Almond paste .... 50 gms / 3 ⅓ tbs
Garam masala, whole .... 10 gms / 2 tsp	Salt to taste
Bayleaf *(tej patta)* 1	White pepper powder .... 3 gms / ½ tsp
Onions, pounded .... 10 gms / 2 tsp	Saffron *(kesar)* .... a few strands
Garlic, chopped............................... 10 gms / 2 tsp	**For garnishing:**
Ginger, chopped .... 10 gms / 2 tsp	Lamb brunoise, boiled .... 50 gms / 3 ⅓ tbs

Method:

1. Soak wheat in sufficient water overnight and squeeze out the wheat milk.

2. Heat water (2 litres / 10 cups) in a handi *(pot)*, add the lamb bones, garam masala, bayleaf, onion, garlic, ginger and allow to cook for about 4-5 hours on low heat. Remove from heat and strain through a soup strainer.

3. Melt butter in a pan and sauté the onions till slightly

browned. Stir in the strained stock, cook for 5-10 minutes.

4. Add the almond paste and allow to cook for 5 minutes. Stir in the salt and white pepper powder. Remove from heat and strain the stock.

5. Reheat the stock in a handi *(pot)*, add saffron and wheat milk. Bring to a boil and remove from heat.

6. Serve hot, garnished with boiled lamb brunoise. (Picture on page 15).

C H I C K E N

Clockwise from left: Murg Daraanpur (page 29), Chicken Badam Pasanda (page 31), Tandoori Kofta (page 33) and Murg Jugalbandi (page 35).

Murg Kandhari

Chicken cooked with pomegranate juice

Serves: 4, Preparation time: 20 minutes, Cooking time: 25 minutes

Ingredients:

Chicken, cut into boneless pieces	*700 gms*
Ginger-garlic paste *(page 13)*	*15 gms / 1 tbs*
Salt	*8 gms / 1 ½ tsp*
Red chilli powder	*4 gms / ¾ tsp*
Oil	*40 ml / 2 ²/3 tbs*
Cashewnut paste	*60 gms / 4 tbs*
Yoghurt	*50 gms / 3 ¹/3 tbs*
Water	*200 ml / 1 cup*
Brown onion paste *(page 13)*	*20 gms / 4 tsp*
Tomato purée *(page 13)*	*40 gms / 2 ²/3 tbs*
Pomegranate *(anardana)* seeds	*100 gms / ½ cups*
Cream	*50 gms / 3 ¹/3 tbs*
Garam masala *(page 13)*	*3 gms / ½ tsp*

Method:

1. Wash, clean and dry the chicken pieces. Marinate the chicken pieces with ginger-garlic paste (2 tsp), half of salt and red chilli powder and keep aside for 10-15 minutes.

2. Heat oil (30 ml) in a pan. Sauté the chicken pieces for a few minutes without letting the colour change. Keep aside.

3. Add the remaining oil to the pan, sauté the remaining ginger-garlic paste for 2-3 minutes. Add cashewnut paste mixed with yoghurt and water. Season with remaining salt and red chilli powder, simmer for 8-10 minutes.

4. Add the brown onion paste, tomato purée and chicken pieces and cook on low heat till the chicken is tender and the curry has thickened.

5. Extract juice from pomegranate seeds and strain through a muslin cloth into the simmering curry.

6. Stir in the cream. Remove from heat, transfer to a serving dish, and serve hot, garnished with garam masala.

Chicken Bannu Kabab

A delicate kabab of chicken cubes with a hint of fenugreek

Serves: 4, Preparation time: 45 minutes, Cooking time: 20 minutes

Ingredients:

Chicken, cut into boneless cubes	*900 gms*
Salt	*10 gms / 2 tsp*
Dry fenugreek *(kasoori methi)* powder	*2 gms / ¹/3 tsp*
Ginger-garlic paste *(page 13)*	*30 gms /2 tbs*
Green chillies, chopped	*10 gms / 2 tsp*
Green coriander, chopped	*10 gms /2 tsp*
Vinegar	*5 gms / 1 tsp*
Oil	*70 gms / 4 ²/3 tbs*
Gramflour *(besan)*, seived	*25 gms / 5 tsp*
Bread crumbs, fresh	*40 gms / 2 ²/3 tbs*
Egg *(yolks only)*, whisked	*6*

Method:

1. Wash and dry the chicken cubes. Add salt, dry fenugreek powder, ginger-garlic paste, green chillies, green coriander alongwith vinegar to the cubes and mix thoroughly. Refrigerate for 15 minutes.

2. Heat oil in a pan, add gramflour and stir-fry till a pleasing smell emanates. Add the chicken cubes and sauté on low heat for 3-5 minutes till they are half cooked.

3. Add breadcrumbs and mix well. Remove and spread on a clean table top. Allow to cool.

4. Skewer the cubes 2" apart and roast in a tandoor till done. Bring the cubes close together and coat with egg yolks.

5. Roast in the tandoor till the egg yolk coating turns golden brown in colour. Remove from the skewer and serve hot, garnished with onion rings and accompained by Mint chutney (page 91). (Picture on page 24).

Neza Kabab

Marinated chicken legs with a distinctive flavour of green cardamom

Serves: 4, Preparation time: 40 minutes, Cooking time: 25 minutes

Ingredients:

Chicken, legs .... *900 gms*	Green coriander, chopped .... *40 gms / 2 ²/₃ tbs*
Ginger-garlic paste *(page 13)* .... *80 gms / 5 ¹/₃ tbs*	Green cardamom *(choti elaichi)* powder . *4 gms / ³/₄ tsp*
Salt .... *8 gms / 1 ½ tsp*	Oil ....*60 ml / 4 tbs*
White pepper powder .... *4 gms / ³/₄ tsp*	Gramflour *(besan)* ....*300 gms / 1 ½ cups*
Garam masala *(page 13)* .... *4 gms / ³/₄ tsp*	Eggs, whisked *4*
Dry fenugreek *(kasoori methi)* powder..... *2 gms / ¹/₃ tsp*	Cream..*200 gms / 1 cup*
Vinegar ....*20 ml / 4 tsp*	Butter for basting

Method:

1. Wash and clean the chicken legs. Remove the thigh bone from the flesh. Take care to see that it is not completely removed.

2. Prepare a marinade by mixing together ginger-garlic paste, salt, white pepper powder, garam masala, dry fenugreek powder, vinegar, green coriander and green cardamom powder. Marinate the chicken legs in this marinade and keep aside for 20 minutes.

3. Heat oil in a pan, add gramflour and stir-fry on low heat till a pleasing smell emanates. Remove from heat and transfer to a mixing bowl and allow to cool.

4. Add 1 egg and blend to make a smooth paste, add cream and mix well.

5. Add the remaining eggs to the mixture and mix thoroughly. Coat the chicken legs with this marinade and keep aside for 20 minutes.

6. Skewer the chicken legs once along the bone and once through the thigh flesh. Cook in a tandoor for about 8-10 minutes or till slightly coloured. Remove and let excess liquids drip.

7. Baste lightly with butter and roast again for 2-3 minutes or till completely done.

8. Remove from skewers onto a serving platter, garnish with lemon wedges, cucumber and tomato dices, onion rings and serve hot.

Murg Daraanpur

Chicken breasts coated with cornflour mixture and deep fried

Serves: 4, Preparation time: 1 hour, Cooking time: 20-30 minutes

Ingredients:

Chicken, breasts *8*	Cashewnuts, chopped .... *50 gms / 3 ¹/₃ tbs*
Red chilli powder...............................*4 gms / ³/₄ tsp*	Green coriander, chopped .... *12 gms / 2 ¹/₃ tsp*
Garam masala *(page 13)* .... *2 gms / ¹/₃ tsp*	Green chillies, chopped .... *10 gms / 2 tsp*
Dry fenugreek *(kasoori methi)* powder............. *a pinch*	**For the batter:**
White pepper powder .... *a pinch*	Cornflour ....*100 gms / ½ cup*
Salt .... *3 gms / ½ tsp*	Water.....................................*300 ml / 1 ½ cups*
Ginger-garlic paste *(page 13)* .... *16 gms / 1 tbs*	Vinegar ....*5 ml / 1 tsp*
Vinegar ....*5 ml / 1 tsp*	Salt .... *a pinch*
Oil ....*10 ml / 2 tsp*	White pepper powder .... *a pinch*
For the filling:	Flour...*65 gms / 4 ¹/₃ tbs*
Cheese, grated..............................*600 gms / 3 cups*	Ginger-garlic paste *(page 13)* ....*8 gms / 1 ½ tsp*
Chicken tikka, cooked, chopped .... *190 gms*	Eggs, whisked *2*
Raisins, chopped ....*50 gms / 3 ¹/₃ tbs*	Oil for frying

Method:

1. Wash, clean and dry the chicken breasts.

2. Mix together red chilli powder, garam masala, dry fenugreek powder, white pepper powder, salt, ginger-garlic paste, vinegar and oil to make a paste.

3. Slit the chicken breasts from the sides, open out and flatten with a steak hammer without rupturing the flesh.

4. Smear the chicken breasts with the prepared paste evenly.

5. Prepare the filling, by mixing together cheese, chicken tikka, raisins, cashewnuts, green coriander and green chillies.

6. Divide the filling into 8 equal portions and place in the

centre of each piece.

7. Roll the pieces firmly over the filling and refrigerate for 10 minutes.

8. Dissolve the cornflour in water to a lump free batter, add vinegar, salt, white pepper powder, flour, ginger-garlic paste and eggs. Mix well.

9. Heat oil in a kadhai *(wok)*, dip each chicken piece in the cornflour batter and deep fry on medium hot oil till half done.

10. Remove and drain excess oil.

11. Just before serving, deep fry the pieces 'daraanpur' until golden brown in colour, remove, cut into half and serve. (Picture on page 25).

Chooza Kabab

Skewered chicken chunks in a highly aromatic and flavourful curry,
served with capsicum and onions on a bed of rice

Serves: 4, Preparation time:45 minutes, Cooking time:15 minutes

Ingredients:

Chicken, cut into boneless pieces .... *900 gms*
Basmati rice .... *300 gms / 1 ½ cup*
Yoghurt .... *10 gms / 2 tsp*
Ginger-garlic paste *(page 13)* .... *30 gms / 2 tbs*
Salt to taste
Curry powder .... *10 gms / 2 tsp*
Tomatos, quartered .... *235 gms / 1¹/₃ cup*
Onions, quartered .... *145 gms / ¾ cup*
Capsicum, quartered .... *90 gms / 6 tbs*
Oil ....*80 ml / 5¹/₃ tbs*
Cumin *(jeera)* seeds .... *2 gms / ¹/₃ tsp*
Black cardamom *(bari elaichi)* *2*
Green cardamom *(choti elaichi)* *2*

Cinnamon *(daalchini)* sticks *2*
Cloves *(laung)*.. *2*
Bayleaves *(tej patta)* *4*
Brown onion paste *(page 13)* .... *125 gms / ½ cup*
Dry coconut, grated .... *35 gms / 2 ¹/₃ tbs*
Turmeric *(haldi)* powder .... *10 gms / 2 tsp*
Red chilli powder .... *3 gms / ½ tsp*
Coriander powder .... *15 gms / 1 tbs*
Tomato purée *(page 13)* .... *100 gms/ ½ cup*
Chicken stock .... *500 ml / 2 ½ cups*
Cream .... *60 gms / 4 tbs*
Green coriander, chopped .... *20 gms / 4 tsp*

Method:

1. Marinate the chicken pieces in yoghurt, ginger-garlic paste (2 tsp), salt (½ tsp), curry powder (½ tsp) and oil (1 tsp). Keep aside for 20 minutes.
2. Clean and soak the rice in water for 20 minutes. Boil in sufficient water until cooked. Remove and keep aside.
3. Skewer the marinated chicken pieces in alternate layers with tomato, onion and capsicum quarters and grill over a hot plate till completely cooked from all sides, basting with oil from time to time. Remove & keep aside.
4. For the curry, heat oil (3¹/₃ tbs) in a pan, add cumin seeds, black cardamom, green cardamom, cinnamon, cloves and bayleaves, saute till they crackle.

5. Stir in the remaining ginger-garlic paste and sauté further for a minute. Add brown onion paste, coconut, turmeric powder, red chilli powder, coriander powder and remaining curry powder. Stir-fry till the oil seperates.
6. Add the tomato purée and cook further for 5 minutes.
7. Stir in the chicken stock and cook till the curry thickens. Stir in cream. Remove from heat and keep aside.
8. On a serving platter, spread the cooked rice. Remove the kabab as well as tomato, onion and capsicum quarters and arrange neatly on top of the rice.
9. Pour the curry on top and serve hot, garnished with chopped coriander.

Chicken Badam Pasanda

Chicken cooked with almond paste and finished in a rich creamy curry.

Serves: 4, Preparation time: 15 minutes, Cooking time: 40 minutes

Ingredients:

Chicken, escalopes .... *600 gms*
Egg, whisked *1*
Salt .... *12 gms / 2 tsp*
Red chilli powder .... *7 gms / 1 ½ tsp*
Lemon juice .... *10 gms / 2 tsp*
Ginger-garlic paste *(page 13)* .... *25 gms / 5 tsp*
Oil for frying .... *10 gms / 2 tsp*
Almonds, blanched .... *70 gms / 4 ²/₃ tbs*
Yoghurt .... *100 gms / ½ cup*
Butter .... *30 gms / 2 tbs*

Ginger-garlic paste *(page 13)* .... *15 gms / 1 tbs*
White pepper powder .... *3 gms / ½ tsp*
Brown onion paste *(page 13)* .... *30 gms / 2 tbs*
Tomato purée *(page 13)* .... *70 gms / 4 ²/₃ tbs*
Cream .... *50 gms / 3 ¹/₃ tbs*

For garnishing:
Garam masala *(page 13)* .... *a pinch*
Cream .... *5 gms / 1 tsp*
Almonds, slivered .... *10 gms / 2 tsp*

Method:

1. For the batter, mix together, egg, salt (1 tsp), red chilli powder (½ tsp), lemon juice and ginger-garlic paste.
2. Flatten out each escalope with a steak hammer and coat with the prepared batter. Refrigerate for 15 minutes.
3. Heat oil in a pan and shallow fry the chicken pieces until golden brown on both sides.
4. Remove from heat, drain excess oil and keep aside.
5. For the curry, grind the almonds to a fine past and blend with yoghurt.
6. Heat oil and butter in a pan, add ginger-garlic paste and sauté for a few seconds. Add yoghurt and sauté, stirring constantly.

7. Stir in the remaining salt and red chilli powder alongwith white pepper powder and cook for a few seconds.
8. Stir in onion paste, tomato purée, cream and sauté for 8-10 minutes. Add chicken pieces to the curry and cook on low heat till the pieces are tender and the curry reduces to half.
9. Remove the chicken pieces from the curry and place neatly on a serving platter, pour the curry on top.
10. Sprinkle garam masala and drizzle cream. Serve hot, garnished with slivered almonds and accompanied by any Indian bread. (Picture on page 25).

Murg Chakori

Minced lamb stuffed chicken breasts, marinated in yoghurt, cooked in a tandoor

Serves: 4, Preparation time: 40 minutes, Cooking time: 30 minutes

Ingredients:

Chicken, breasts 8	Asafoetida *(heeng)* .... *a pinch*
Lamb, minced .... *250 gms*	Oil .... *200 ml / 1 cup*
Black cumin *(shah jeera)* .... *2 gms / 1/3 tsp*	Water .... *200 ml / 1 cup*
Dry ginger *(sonth)* powder .... *5 gms / 1 tsp*	**For the marinade:**
Fennel *(saunf)* powder .... *10 gms / 2 tsp*	Yoghurt, drained .... *500 gms / 2 ½ cup*
Cumin *(jeera)* powder .... *5 gms / 1 tsp*	Salt to taste
Red chilli powder .... *5 gms / 1 tsp*	Cream .... *100 ml / ½ cup*
Coriander powder .... *5 gms / 1 tsp*	Red chilli powder .... *5 gms / 1 tsp*
Salt .... *10 gms / 2 tsp*	Vinegar .... *8 ml / 1 ½ tsp*
Yoghurt .... *50 gms / 3 1/3 tbs*	Coriander powder .... *5 gms / 1 tsp*

Method:

1. Clean the chicken breasts, slit open from one side and flatten. Keep aside.

2. Blend together the lamb mince, black cumin, dry ginger powder, fennel powder, cumin powder, red chilli powder, coriander powder, salt, yoghurt and asafoetida.

3. Divide the mince mixture into even size balls. In a pan, heat oil and water in equal quantities, reduce heat and immerse the balls into the pan. Cover and cook for about 20 minutes.

4. Stuff the prepared 'koftas' meat balls into the chicken breasts. Place the chicken breasts over silver foil and wrap firmly. Poach for 15 minutes.

5. Remove from heat and unwrap the chicken breast from the foil and allow to cool.

6. For the marinade, blend yoghurt alongwith salt, cream, red chilli powder, vinegar and coriander powder. Keep aside.

7. Marinate the chicken breasts with the prepared marinade and keep aside for 15 minutes.

8. Skewer the chicken breasts and cook in a tandoor for 5-10 minutes or until golden yellow in colour.

9. Remove from the skewers and serve hot, accompanied by Tandoori roti (Page 95).

Tandoori Kofta

Chicken breasts with an exotic filling roasted in a tandoor or in an oven

Serves: 4, Preparation time: 30 minutes, Cooking time: 30-40 minutes

Ingredients:

Chicken, breasts 8	Green coriander, chopped .... *3 gms / ½ tsp*
Chicken, minced .... *225 gms*	Water .... *1 litre / 5 cups*
Fenugreek *(methi)* powder .... *2 gms / 1/3 tsp*	Yoghurt, drained .... *200 gms / 1 cup*
Garam masala *(page 13)* .... *2 gms / 1/3 tsp*	Cream .... *80 gms / 5 1/3 tbs*
White pepper powder .... *7 gms / 1 1/3 tsp*	Saffron *(kesar)* .... *a few strands*
Green cardamom *(choti elaichi)* powder ... *5 gms / 1 tsp*	Oil .... *30 ml / 2 tbs*
Salt to taste	Red chilli powder .... *a pinch*
Lemon juice .... *5 ml / 1 tsp*	Ginger-garlic paste *(page 13)* .... *30 gms / 2 tbs*
Green chillies, chopped 2	

Method:

1. Mix half of the fenugreek powder, garam masala, white pepper powder, green cardamom powder, salt, lemon juice, in the chicken mince. Add green chillis and green coriander. Shape into 8 equal round balls and keep aside for 5 minutes.

2. Beat the chicken breast with hammer and put one ball in each breast. Make a round shape alongwith the breast keeping the wing bone standing straight.

3. Wrap it tightly with aluminium foil like a ball.

4. Boil water in a container and cook the chicken breasts in it covered with a lid for 15 minutes.

5. Drain excess water and place the chicken breasts under running water for 1 minute.

6. Make a second marinade of remaining lemon juice, yoghurt, cream, saffron, oil, salt, red chilli powder and ginger-garlic paste.

7. Marinate the chicken breasts in the second marinade for 5 minutes.

8. Skewer and roast for about 10 minutes in a hot tandoor or in a hot oven (approx 350° F).

9. Remove from skewers and serve hot, garnished with onion rings and lemon wedges and accompanied by Mint chutney (Page 91). (Picture on page 25).

Tandoori Chicken Chaat

An appetiser of sliced tandoori chicken in a spicy masala with a touch of raw mango

Serves: 4, Preparation time: 10 minutes, Cooking time: 10 minutes

Ingredients:

Tandoori chicken, shredded 2	Onions, finely sliced .... *100 gms / ½ cup*
Lemon juice .... *15 ml / 1 tbs*	Green chillies, chopped .... *10 gms / 2 tsp*
Salt to taste	Green coriander, chopped .... *40 gms / 2 ⅔ tbs*
Red chilli powder .... *2 gms / ⅓ tsp*	Chaat masala .... *10 gms / 2 tsp*
Oil .... *15 ml / 1 tbs*	Ginger, chopped .... *5 gms / 1 tsp*
Raw green mango .... *100 gms / ½ cup*	

Method:

1. Prepare a lemon dressing by mixing together the lemon juice alongwith salt, red chilli powder and oil. Keep aside.
2. Cut the raw mango into strips.
3. In a mixing bowl, add mango, onions, green chillies, green coriander, chaat masala alongwith the shredded chicken and the lemon dressing. Mix well.
4. Remove to a serving bowl and serve immediately, garnished with chopped ginger.

Murg Jugalbandi

Chicken breasts stuffed with a filling of chicken mince mixture in a thick curry

Serves: 4, Preparation time: 15 minutes, Cooking time: 1 hour

Ingredients:

Chicken breasts 8	Cumin *(jeera)* Seeds .... *a pinch*
For the filling:	Ginger-garlic paste *(page 13)* .... *10 gms / 2 tsp*
Chicken, minced .... *200 gms*	Salt to taste
Oil .... *10 ml / 2 tsp*	Red chilli powder .... *2 gms / ⅓ tsp*
Mustard *(raee)* seeds .... *2 gms / ⅓ tsp*	Turmeric *(haldi)* powder .... *3 gms / ½ tsp*
Curry leaves .... *2 gms / ⅓ tsp*	Coriander powder .... *5 gms / 1 tsp*
Salt .... *2 gms / ⅓ tsp*	Yoghurt, whisked .... *50 gms / 3 ⅓ tbs*
Red chilli powder .... *2 gms / ⅓ tsp*	Tomato purée *(page 13)* .... *50 gms / 3 ⅓ tbs*
Garam masala *(page 13)* .... *2 gms / ⅓ tsp*	Brown onion paste *(page 13)* .... *50 gms / 3 ⅓ tbs*
Coconut, fresh, grated .... *10 gms / 2 tsp*	Water .... *80 ml / 1 cup*
Oil for frying	Tomato, diced 1
For the curry:	Green peppercorns .... *4 gms / ¾ tsp*
Oil .... *20 ml / 4 tsp*	

Method:

1. Clean and wash the chicken breasts. Make deep incisions near the bone of the chicken breast, Keep aside.
2. Heat oil in a pan, add mustard seeds and curry leaves, sauté for a few seconds, add the mince and cook for about 5-6 minutes.
3. Add salt, red chilli powder and garam masala alongwith grated coconut, stir and cook for a few minutes. Remove from heat and keep aside to cool.
4. Stuff the chicken breasts with the prepared mixture. Heat oil in a pan, add 2 chicken breasts at a time and sauté till golden brown on both sides. Remove and keep aside.
5. For the curry, heat oil in a pan, add cumin and sauté for a few seconds, add ginger-garlic paste and sauté for

1 minute.
6. Add salt, red chilli powder, turmeric powder and coriander powder and cook for a minute.
7. Stir in the yoghurt and tomato purée and stir-fry on medium heat, add the brown onion paste and cook till oil leaves the sides. Add water and bring to a boil, simmer and cook till the curry reduces to ¾ th.
8. Add the chicken pieces to the curry and allow to cook for 10-12 minutes. Remove from heat.
9. Carefully lift the chicken pieces from the curry and place onto a serving platter. Pour the curry on top and serve hot, garnished with tomato dices and green peppercorns and accompanied by any Indian bread. (Picture on page 25).

Tangri kabab

Chicken drumsticks cooked in a tandoor, coated with egg and cashewnut mixture.

Serves: 4, Preparation time: 1 hour, Cooking time: 15-20 minutes

Ingredients:

Chicken, drumsticks 12
Ginger-garlic paste *(page 13)* .... 20 gms / 4 tsp
White pepper powder .... a pinch
Salt .... 4 gms / 3/4 tsp
Vinegar .... 5 ml / 1 tsp
Yoghurt .... 250 gms / 1 1/3 cups
Cream .... 150 gms / 2/3 cup
Ginger-garlic paste *(page 13)* .... 30 gms / 2 tbs

White pepper powder .... 2 gms / 1/3 tsp
Garam masala *(page 13)* .... 4 gms / 3/4 tsp
Salt .... 2 gms / 1/3 tsp
Saffron *(kesar)* .... a few strands
Oil for basting
Eggs, whisked 4
Cashewnuts, finely ground .... 75 gms / 5 tbs

Method:

1. Wash and clean the chicken drumsticks. Make 4-5 deep vertical incisions.
2. Mix ginger-garlic paste, white pepper powder, salt and vinegar to make a paste. Coat the drumsticks with this paste and rub into the slits. Refrigerate for 15 minutes.
3. Make a second marinade with yoghurt, cream, ginger-garlic paste, white pepper powder, garam masala, salt and saffron.
4. Marinate the chicken in the prepared marinade and

refrigerate for another 15 minutes.
5. Skewer the drumsticks and roast in a tandoor for 3-5 minutes till half cooked. Remove and hang for 2-3 minutes.
6. Baste with oil and roast till completely cooked.
7. Mix together the ground cashewnut and eggs. Coat the drumsticks and roast again till the egg has coagulated.
8. Remove and serve hot.

Murg Aloo Bukhara

Chicken dumplings stuffed with dried plums in an exotic curry

Serves: 4, Preparation time: 30 minutes, Cooking time: 45 minutes

Ingredients:

For the Dumplings:
Chicken, minced .... 1 kg
Cumin *(jeera)* powder .... 3 gms / 1/2 tsp
Black cumin *(shah jeera)* powder .... a pinch
Black cardamom *(bari elaichi)* powder .... 3 gms / 1/2 tsp
Asafoetida *(heeng)* .... 2 gms / 1/3 tsp
Red chilli powder .... 5 gms / 1 tsp
Fennel *(saunf)* seeds .... 6 gms / 1 tsp
Mustard oil .... 40 gms / 2 2/3 tbs
For the filling:
Dried aloo bukhara 16
For the curry:
Mustard oil .... 100 gms / 1/2 cup
Cloves *(laung)* 4

Red chilli powder .... 16 gms / 1 tbs
Water .... 1½ litre / 7 cups
Green cardamom *(choti elaichi)* 4
Black cardamom *(bari elaichi)* 4
Bay leaves *(tej patta)* 2
Black cumin *(shah jeera)* .... a pinch
Salt .... 16 gms / 1 tbs
Turmeric *(haldi)* powder .... 10 gms / 2 tsp
Black cardamom *(bari elaichi)* powder ... 10 gms / 2 tsp
Fennel *(saunf)* powder .... 6 gms / 1 tsp
Cinnamom *(daalchini)* powder .... 6 gms / 1 tsp
Tomatoes, chopped .... 200 gms / 1 cup
Dry ginger powder *(sonth)* .... 2 gms / 1/3 tsp

Method:

1. For the dumplings, mix together all the ingredients and divide into 16 equal portions.
2. Place one aloo bukhara in the centre of each portion. Shape into balls and keep aside.
3. For the curry, heat mustard oil in a handi *(pot)* till it begins to smoke, add cloves and sauté till they crackle. Reduce heat to low.
4. Add the red chilli powder, allow to infuse, stir in water

and bring to a boil.
5. Add the remaining whole and powdered spices and condiments and bring to a boil. Reduce heat to low and gently add the chicken balls to the simmering curry.
6. Allow to cook for 25-30 minutes till the chicken balls are cooked and the curry thickens. Remove from heat and transfer to a serving dish.
7. Serve hot, accompanied by Tandoori roti (Page 95).

FISH & SEAFOOD

Clockwise from left: Jhinga Mehrunisa (page 43), Saloni Fish Tikka (page 45), Jhinga Til Tikka (page 43) and Tandoori Pomfret (page 45).

Jalpari Kabab

Saffron flavoured fish rolls stuffed with prawns

Serves:4, Preparation time: 40 minutes, Cooking time: 20 minutes

Ingredients:

Fish fillets, thin 12	Red chilli powder .... *5 gms / 1 tsp*
Prawns, shelled, deveined .... *220 gms*	Lemon juice .... *5 gms / 1 tsp*
Ginger-garlic paste *(page 13)* .... *25 gms / 5 tsp*	Oil .... *20 ml / 4 tsp*
Mango pickle masala .... *25 gms / 5 tsp*	Yoghurt, drained .... *180 gms / 3/4 cup*
Carom *(ajwain)* seeds .... *2 gms / 1/3 tsp*	Cream .... *30 gms / 2 tbs*
White pepper powder .... *5 gms / 1 tsp*	Saffron *(kesar)* .... *a few strands*
Garam masala *(page 13)* .... *4 gms / 3/4 tsp*	Green cardamom *(choti elaichi)* powder .... *a pinch*
Salt to taste	Water .... *1 ltr / 5 cups*

Method:

1. Extract juice from ginger-garlic paste and keep aside.
2. Clean the fish fillets and prawns. Pat dry with a cloth.
3. Make a marinade with half of the carom seeds, white pepper powder, garam masala, salt, red chilli powder, lemon juice, extract of ginger-garlic paste, pickle masala and oil.
4. Marinate the fish fillets in the prepared marinade and keep aside for 5 minutes.
5. Prepare second marinade of yoghurt, cream, saffron, green cardamom powder and the remaining half of other ingredients. Keep it aside.
6. Put one fish fillet flat on a table top. Place a prawn at one end of the fillet and roll the fillet. Wrap it tightly with cling wrap or aluminium foil.
7. Boil water in a handi *(pot)* and cook the rolls for 10 minutes keeping the pot covered.
8. Drain the water and place the rolls under running water for 1 minute. Remove the foil.
9. Marinate the rolls in the second marinade for 5 minutes.
10. Skewer the rolls and roast it in hot tandoor or in an oven (approx 300-350°F) for 10 minutes.
11. Remove from skewers, transfer to a serving platter and serve hot, accompanied by Mint chutney (Page 91).

Maccher Jhol

Mustard flavoured bengali fish curry

Serves:4, Preparation time:20 minutes, Cooking time: 40 minutes

Ingredients:

Pomfret .... *900 gms*	Ginger-garlic paste *(page 13)* .... *20 gms / 4 tsp*
Turmeric *(haldi)* powder .... *5 gms / 1 tsp*	Tomatoes, finely chopped .... *100 gms / 1/2 cup*
Salt .... *10 gms / 2 tsp*	Green chillies, sliced .... *10 gms / 2 tsp*
Oil .... *for frying*	Red chilli powder .... *4 gms / 3/4 tsp*
Fenugreek *(methi dana)* seeds .... *2 gms / 1/3 tsp*	Coriander powder .... *6 gms / 1 1/3 tsp*
Cumin *(jeera)* seeds .... *3 gms / 1/2 tsp*	Water .... *500 ml / 2 1/2 cups*
Bayleaves *(tej patta)* 4	Green coriander, chopped .... *5 gms / 1 tsp*
Onions, finely chopped .... *200 gms / 1 cup*	

Method:

1. Wash and clean the fish, remove the head and tail and cut into pieces.
2. Apply half of turmeric powder and salt on the fish pieces and keep aside.
3. Heat oil in a pan and shallow fry the fish on both sides till ¾ done. Remove and keep aside.
4. In the same pan, add fenugreek and cumin seeds, sauté till they crackle, add bayleaves, onions and stir-fry to a golden brown colour on medium heat.
5. Add the ginger-garlic paste, stir-fry for a minute, add tomatoes and cook till the oil separates.
6. Add green chillies, remaining salt, red chilli powder and coriander powder.
7. Cook on a low heat for 2-3 minutes, increase heat, add water and bring to a boil.
8. Add the fish pieces and simmer.
9. Cover and cook for 10-15 minutes, till the fish is completely cooked and the curry has thickened.
10. Remove from heat onto a serving dish and serve hot, garnished with chopped coriander. (Picture on page 38).

Prawn Malai Curry

Sea fresh prawns cooked in a lip smacking curry

Serves:4, Preparation time:10 minutes , Cooking time:30 minutes

Ingredients:

Prawns, shelled, deveined	16	Curry leaves	5 gms / 1 tsp
Coconut, fresh, grated	1	Salt to taste	
Oil	50 ml / 3 $^{1/3}$ tbs	Yoghurt, whisked	50 gms / 3 $^{1/3}$ tbs
Ginger-garlic paste *(page 13)*	10 gms / 2 tsp	Tomato purée *(page 13)*	50 gms / 3 $^{1/3}$ tbs
Red chilli powder	5 gms / 1 tsp	Water	200 ml / 1 cup
Coriander powder	5 gms / 1 tsp	Garam masala *(page 13)*	2 gms / $^{1/3}$ tsp
Turmeric *(haldi)* powder	5 gms / 1 tsp		

Method:

1. Squeeze out the milk from the grate coconut and strain through a muslin cloth. Keep aside.
2. Heat oil in a handi *(pot)*, add all the ingredients except yoghurt and tomato purée. Stir-fry for 2-3 minutes.
3. Stir in the yoghurt and tomato purée, mix well and cook for about 5-7 minutes.
4. Add prawns and stir-fry for 2-3 minutes. Add water to allow the prawns to cook till they are tender and curry thickens, stir in garam masala and coconut milk. Remove from heat and serve, accompanied by steamed rice.

Prawn Mehrunisa

Prawns coated in a rich and creamy marinade, cooked in a tandoor

Serves: 4, Preparation time: 40 minutes, Cooking time: 10 minutes

Ingredients:

Prawns, shelled, deveined	1400 gms	Cheese, grated	80 gms / 5 $^{1/3}$ tbs
Vinegar	40 ml / 2 $^{2/3}$ tbs	Dry fenugreek *(kasoori methi)* powder	4 gms / ¾ tsp
Salt to taste		Ginger-garlic paste *(page 13)*	40 gms / 2 $^{2/3}$ tbs
Lemon juice	20 ml / 4 tsp	Garam masala *(page 13)*	8 gms / 1 ½ tsp
Yoghurt	240 gms / 1 $^{1/3}$ cup	Saffron *(kesar)*	a few strands
Cream	200 gms / 1 cup	Butter for basting	
White pepper powder	8 gms / 1 ½ tsp		

Method:

1. Wash the prawns with vinegar and salt water. Drain and pat dry.
2. Prepare a marinade by mixing together all the ingredients except butter.
3. Marinate the prawns in the prepared marinade and keep aside for 30 minutes.
4. Skewer the prawns and roast in a moderately hot tandoor for 6-8 minutes. Remove from tandoor and allow excess liquids to drip.
5. Baste lightly with butter and roast again for 2-3 minutes. Remove from skewers and serve, accompanied by Mint chutney (page 91). (Picture on page 39).

Jhinga Til Tikka

Sesame seed coated fried prawns with flavours of Indian spices

Serves: 4, Preparation time: 1 hour, Cooking time: 15 minutes

Ingredients:

Prawns, shelled, deveined	1 kg	Carom *(ajwain)* seeds	8 gms / 1 ½ tsp
Ginger paste *(page 13)*	25 gms / 5 tsp	Cream	60 gms / 4 tbs
Garlic paste *(page 13)*	30 gms / 2 tbs	Mace *(javitri)* powder	3 gms / ½ tsp
White pepper powder	3 gms / ½ tsp	Green cardamom *(choti elaichi)* powder	2 gms / $^{1/3}$ tsp
Red chilli powder	3 gms / ½ tsp	Blackgram *(chana)* roasted, powdered	30 gms / 2 tbs
Salt to taste		Eggs	4
Lemon juice	60 ml / 4 tbs	Seasame *(til)* seeds	50 gms / 3 $^{2/3}$ tbs
Cheese, grated	60 gms / 4 tbs	Oil for frying	
Yoghurt, drained	120 gms / ½ cup		

Method:

1. Mix together ginger paste, garlic paste, white pepper powder, red chilli powder, salt and lemon juice. Marinate the prawns in this mixture and keep aside for 30 minutes.
2. Mix the cheese into the yoghurt along with all the other ingredients except blackgram powder and sesame seeds. Coat the prawns with the cheese mixture and keep aside for 30 minutes
3. In a separate bowl, mix the blackgram powder and sesame seeds, lightly dust the prawns with this mixture and deep fry in hot oil until golden brown in colour.
4. Remove, drain excess oil and serve hot, accompanied by Coriander chutney (page 89). (Picture on page 39).

Saloni Fish Tikka

Fish cooked in a delightful marinade of Indian spices

Serves: 4, Preparation time: 40 minutes, Cooking time: 15-20 minutes

Ingredients:

Fish, cut into boneless pieces .... 800 gms	Ginger-garlic paste *(page 13)* .... 25 gms / 5 tsp
Salt .... 15 gms / 1 tbs	Yoghurt, drained .... 10 gms / 2 tsp
White pepper powder .... 5 gms / 1 tsp	Vinegar.. 150 ml / 3/4 cup
Fenugreek *(methi)* powder .... 3 gms / ½ tsp	Cream.. 100 gms / ½ cup
Turmeric *(haldi)* powder .... 3 gms / ½ tsp	Mustard oil .... 60 ml / 4 tbs
Red chilli powder.................................. 8 gms / 1 ½ tsp	Cloves 16
Garam masala *(page 13)* .... 2 gms / 1/3 tsp	Charcoal piece, live 1
Clove *(laung)* powder .... a pinch	Oil for basting

Method:

1. Wash, clean and dry the fish pieces.

2. Prepare a marinade by mixing together salt, white pepper powder, dry fenugreek powder, turmeric powder, red chilli powder, garam masala, clove powder, ginger-garlic paste, yoghurt, vinegar and cream.

3. Marinate the fish pieces in the prepared marinade and keep in a bowl.

4. Make a well in the centre and put mustard oil and cloves in it. Place the live charcoal piece in the oil and cover the bowl with a lid. Seal the lid so that the smoke does not escape. Keep aside for 30 minutes.

5. Remove the lid, skewer the fish piece and roast in a medium hot tandoor for 5-6 minutes. Remove, from the tandoor and allow excess liquids to drip.

6. Baste with oil and roast again for 2 minutes until done. Remove from skewers and transfer to a serving platter.

7. Serve hot, accompanied by a green salad and Coriander chutney (page 89).

Tandoori Pomfret

Whole pomfret marinated in fine Indian herbs and cooked in a tandoor

Serves:4, Preparation time: 30 minutes, Cooking time: 10-15 minutes

Ingredients:

Pomfret .... 4 / 1600 gms	Yoghurt, thick .... 500 gms / 2 ½ cups
Ginger-garlic paste *(page 13)* .... 120 gms / 1 1/3 cup	Carom *(ajwain)* seeds .... 6 gms / 1 tsp
Salt .... 20 gms / 4 tsp	Dry fenugreek *(kasoori methi)* powder...... 6 gms / 1 tsp
Red chilli powder...................................... 20 gms / 4 tsp	Oil for basting
Garam masala *(page 13)* .... 12 gms / 2 1/3 tsp	

Method:

1. Discard the fins from the pomfrets. Clean the stomach and wash the fish thoroughly.

2. Make incisions ½ " apart on both sides of the pomfrets.

3. Mix together half of ginger-garlic paste, salt, red chilli powder and garam masala. Rub this mixture onto the fish and the slits. Keep aside for 15-20 minutes.

4. Prepare a marinade by mixing the remaining half of ginger-garlic paste, salt, red chilli powder and garam masala alongwith yoghurt, carom seeds and dry fenugreek powder. Marinate the pomfrets in the prepared marinade.

5. Skewer the pomfrets and roast in a medium hot tandoor for 8-10 minutes. Remove from tandoor and allow excess liquids to drip.

6. Brush with oil and roast again for 5-7 minutes.

7. Remove from skewers and serve immediately, garnished with onion rings and lemon wedges and accompanied by Mint chutney (page 91). (Picture on page 39).

L A M B

Clockwise from left: Shahi Shikampuri Kabab (page 51),
Sakhat Kabab (page 53), Gosht ki Nihari (page 53) and
Laziz Pasliyan (page 49)

Baoli Handi

A delicacy of lamb, mushrooms and vegetables cooked in a traditional handi.
Serves: 4, Preparation Time: 20 minutes, Cooking Time: 1 hour

Ingredients:

Lamb, cut into boneless cubes .... 900 gms	Coriander powder .... 8 gms / 1½ tsp
Oil .... 125 ml / ²/3 cup	Turmeric *(haldi)* powder .... 5 gms / 1 tsp
Cinnamon *(daalchini)* sticks 2	Tomato purée, fresh *(page 13)* .... 200 gms / 1 cup
Cloves *(laung)* 5	Khoya, grated *(page 13)* .... 30 gms / 2 tbs
Nutmeg *(jaiphal)* 1	Yoghurt... 50 gms / 3¹/3 tbs
Green cardamom *(choti elaichi)* 4	Onion paste, browned *(page 13)* .... 40 gms / 2½ tbs
Ginger-garlic paste *(page 13)* .... 40 gms / 2½ tbs	Green peas, shelled .... 100 gms / ½ cup
Onions, chopped .... 200 gms / 1 cup	Carrots, cut into rounds .... 200 gms / 1 cup
Salt to taste	Mushroom, stems removed .... 80 gms / ¹/3 cup
Red chilli powder.................................... 6 gms / 1 tsp	Cashewnuts, whole .... 150 gms / ²/3 cup
Garam masala *(page 13)*....................... 4 gms / ³/4 tsp	Water.. 800 ml / 4 cups

Method:

1. Heat oil in a handi *(pot)*, add the whole spices and sauté till they crackle, add ginger-garlic paste and sauté for 3-5 minutes.
2. Add the lamb cubes and onions. Cook on medium heat, until moisture dries out. Add salt and all the spices.
3. Stir in tomato purée and cook till it leaves oil.

4. Mix in all the remaining ingredients. Stir for a few seconds and add water.
5. Reduce heat and cook till the lamb pieces are tender and the curry thickens. Remove from heat.
6. Transfer to a serving dish and serve hot, accompanied by Naan (page 95).

Shola Kabab

Spicy and aromatic lamb chunks cooked in tandoor.
Serves: 4, Preparation time: 2 hours, Cooking time: 15-20 minutes

Ingredients:

Lamb, cut into boneless pieces .... 900 gms	Mustard *(raee)* seeds, crushed .... a pinch
Salt .... 16 gms / 1 tbs	Cumin *(jeera)* seeds, crushed .... a pinch
Red chilli powder.................................... 8 gms / 1½ tsp	Coriander seeds, crushed .... a pinch
White pepper powder .... a pinch	Ginger-garlic paste *(page 13)* .... 35 gms / 2¹/3 tbs
Fenugreek *(methi)* powder .... a pinch	Raw papaya, grated .... 60 gms / 4 tbs
Green cardamom *(choti elaichi)* powder .... a pinch	Mustard oil.. 100 ml / ½ cup
Garam masala *(page 13)*........................... 4 gms / ³/4 tsp	Vinegar .... 20 ml / 4 tsp
Onion *(kalonji)* seeds, crushed .... 4 gms / ¾ tsp	Yoghurt... 100 gms / ½ cup
Fennel *(saunf)* seeds, crushed......................... a pinch	Butter for basting .... 20 gms / 4 tsp

Method:

1. Wash, clean and dry the lamb pieces.
2. Prepare a marinade by mixing together all the ingredients.
3. Marinate the lamb pieces in the prepared marinade and keep aside for 1 hour 30 minutes.

4. Skewer the marinated lamb pieces and roast in a medium hot tandoor for 10-12 minutes.
5. Baste with butter and roast again for 5 minutes. Remove from skewers and serve hot, accompanied by Coriander chutney (page 89). (Picture on page 46).

Laziz Pasliyan

Cashewnut flavoured spicy lamb chops
Serves: 4, Preparation time: 30 minutes, Cooking time: 1 hour

Ingredients:

Lamb chops, cleaned 16	Garam masala *(page 13)*........................... 15 gms / 1 tbs
Clarified butter *(ghee)* / Oil .... 200 gms / 1 cup	Coriander powder .... 15 gms / 1 tbs
Onions, chopped .... 500 gms / 2½ cups	Red chilli powder.................................... 15 gms / 1 tbs
Green cardamom *(choti elaichi)* 10	Turmeric *(haldi)* powder .... 3 gms / ½ tsp
Cloves *(laung)*... 4	Salt to taste
Cinnammon *(daalchini)* sticks 4	Cashewnut paste .... 100 gms / ½ cup
Bayleaves *(tej patta)* 2	Yoghurt... 225 gms / 1¼ cup
Ginger-garlic paste *(page 13)* .... 30 gms / 2 tbs	Ginger, julienned .... 20 gms / 4 tsp
Tomatoes, chopped .... 700 gms / 3½ cups	Green coriander, chopped .... 20 gms / 4 tsp

Method:

1. Heat clarified butter/oil in a kadhai *(wok)*, add onions and sauté over medium heat.
2. Add all the ingredients and mix well. Add cashewnut paste, stir-fry until the oil seperates. Stir in the yoghurt.

3. Add lamb chops, cover and cook, stirring occasionally until the lamb chops are tender and curry thickens.
4. Serve hot, garnished with julienned ginger and chopped coriander. (Picture on page 47).

Kallan Kabab

*Skewered rolls of finely chopped lamb liver and kidney covered with chicken mince
and roasted over a charcoal grill*

Serves: 4, Preparation time: 1 hour, Cooking time: 20-25 minutes.

Ingredients:

Lamb, minced .... 250 gms / 1 ¼ cup	Green chillies, chopped .... 5 gms / 1 tsp
Lamb kidney, finely chopped .... 125 gms / ²/3 cup	Chicken, minced .... 500 gms / 2½ cups
Lamb liver, finely chopped.................. 125 gms / ²/3 cup	Salt .... 3 gms / ½ tsp
Salt .... 3 gms / ½ tsp	White pepper powder .... 3 gms / ½ tsp
Red chilli powder................................ 4 gms / ¾ tsp	Garam masala *(page 13)*.......................... a pinch
Garam masala *(page 13)*.................... 2 gms / ¹/3 tsp	Fenugreek *(methi)* powder .... a pinch
Fenugreek *(methi)* powder .... a pinch	Ginger-garlic paste *(page 13)*..................... 2 gms / ¹/3 tsp
Ginger-garlic paste *(page 13)*.................. 10 gms / 2 tsp	Green coriander, chopped .... 4 gms / ¾ tsp
Green coriander, chopped .... 5 gms / 1 tsp	Butter for basting .... 20 gms / 4 tsp

Method:

1. Mix together the lamb mince, kidney, liver, salt, red chilli powder, garam masala, fenugreek powder, ginger-garlic paste, green coriander and green chillies. Keep aside.

2. Skewer the lamb mince mixture and roast in a charcoal grill for 8-10 minutes. Remove from the charcoal grill, place skewer upright to allow excess liquids to drip. Keep aside for 3-5 minutes.

3. Meanwhile, mix chicken mince alongwith all the other ingredients.

4. Apply a coating of the chicken mince mixture evenly onto the lamb mince kababs and roast again for 5-6 minutes.

5. Baste with butter and remove the kababs from skewers in 4 equal portions.

6. Serve immediately, accompained by a green salad and Mint chutney (page 91).

Shahi Shikampuri Kabab

Stuffed minced lamb balls in an exotic curry.

Serves: 4, Preparation time: 45 minutes, Cooking time: 35 minutes

Ingredients:

Lamb, minced .... 500 gms	Onions, chopped .... 50 gms / 3 ¹/3 tbs
Water.................................... 400 ml / 2 cup	Raisins, chopped .... 25 gms / 5 tsp
Lentils *(chana daal)* .... 50 gms / 3 ¹/3 tbs	Oil for frying..250 ml / 1 ¹/3 cup
Cloves *(laung)* powder .... 2 gms / ¹/3 tsp	**For the curry:**
Cinnamon *(daalchini)* powder................... 2 gms / ¹/3 tsp	Oil .... 15 ml / 1 tbs
Green cardamom *(choti elachi)* powder ... 2 gms / ¹/3 tsp	Cumin *(jeera)* powder .... a pinch
Black cardamom *(bari elaichi)* powder .... 2 gms / ¹/3 tsp	Ginger-garlic paste *(page 13)*.................... 10 gms / 2 tsp
Mace *(javitri)* .... a pinch	Salt .... 4 gms / 1 tsp
Salt .... 4 gms / 1 tsp	Red chilli powder............................ 2 gms / ¹/3 tsp
Red chilli powder............................ 5 gm / 1 tsp	Turmeric *(haldi)* powder .... 3 gms / ½ tsp
Ginger-garlic paste *(page 13)* .... 20 gms / 4 tsp	Coriander powder .... 5 gms / 1 tsp
Egg, whisked 1	Yoghurt, whisked.............................. 50 gms / 3¹/3 tbs
For the filling:	Tomato purée *(page 13)*....................... 50 gms / 3¹/3 tbs
Green chillies, chopped .... 5 gms / 1 tsp	Brown onion paste *(page 13)* .... 50 gms / 3¹/3 tbs
Green coriander, chopped .... 5 gms / 1 tsp	Almond paste .... 50 gms /3¹/3 tbs
Ginger, chopped .... 5 gms / 1 tsp	Water.. 300 ml / 1½ cups

Method:

1. Heat water in a handi *(pot)*, add the mince, lentils, whole spices, salt, red chilli powder, ginger-garlic paste and cook for 20-25 minutes or till the water dries up. Remove from heat.

2. Mix in the egg and divide into 16 equal portions.

3. For the filling, mix together all the ingredients. Divide into 16 equal portions. Place one portion of filling over one portion of the mince mixture and shape into a ball. Similarly, prepare the other balls.

4. Heat oil in a kadhai *(wok)* and deep fry the balls a few at a time, till golden brown on all sides. Drain excess oil and keep aside.

5. Heat oil in a pan, add cumin and sauté till they crackle, add ginger-garlic paste and stir-fry for a minute. Add salt, red chilli powder, turmeric powder and coriander powder, cook for a minute.

6. Stir in the yoghurt, tomato purée and brown onion paste, cook on medium heat for 3-4 minutes.

7. Add almond paste and cook till oil separates. Add water, bring to a boil and cook till curry reduces to ¾ th.

8. Add the fried kababs to the curry and mix well. Cook for a few minutes. Remove from heat.

9. Transfer onto a serving platter and serve hot, accompanied by any Indian bread. (Picture on page 47).

Sakhat Kabab

Lamb kababs stuffed with cheese, coated with conflour batter and deep fried.

Serves: 4, Preparation time: 40 minutes, Cooking time: 20-25 minutes

Ingredients:

Lamb, minced	*900 gms*
Salt	*5 gms / 1 tsp*
White pepper powder	*a pinch*
Red chilli powder	*3 gms / ½ tsp*
Fenugreek *(methi)* powder	*a pinch*
Ginger-garlic paste *(page 13)*	*30 gms / 2 tbs*
Green chillies, chopped	*8 gms / 1½ tsp*
Green coriander, chopped	*15 gms / 1 tbs*

For the filling:

Processed cheese, grated	*130 gms / ¾ cup*
Green chillies, chopped	*20 gms / 4 tsp*

For the batter:

Cornflour	*70 gms / 4 ⅔ tbs*
Flour	*70 gms / 4 ⅔ tbs*
Egg, whisked	*1*
Vinegar	*5 ml / 1 tsp*
Salt	*to taste*
White pepper powder	*a pinch*
Ginger-garlic paste *(page 13)*	*8 gms / 1½ tsp*
Water	*300 ml / 1½ cup*
Oil for frying	

Method:

1. Mix the lamb mince alongwith salt, white pepper powder, red chilli powder, garam masala, fenugreek powder, ginger-garlic paste, green chillies, green coriander. Refrigerate for 15 minutes.

2. Mix together the green chillies and cheese. Divide into 16 equal portions.

3. For the batter, mix cornflour alongwith flour, egg, vinegar, salt, white pepper powder, ginger-garlic paste and water.

4. Make 10 cm long kababs with the mince mixture and skewer in 4 equal parts. Roast in a tandoor for 5 minutes and remove. Allow to cool, remove from skewers in 4 pieces each.

5. Slit each kabab lengthwise and stuff the cheese mixture.

6. Dip the stuffed kababs in the prepared batter and deep fry in hot oil until crisp and golden brown in colour.

7. Remove, drain excess oil and serve hot, accompanied by Mint chutney (page 91).

Gosht Ki Nihari

Lamb cooked in a traditional nihari masala on low heat to infuse together the flavours.

Serves: 4, Preparation time: 30 minutes, Cooking time: 1 hour

Ingredients:

Lamb, cut into pieces	*1 kg*
Oil	*200 ml / 1 cup*
Green cardamom *(choti elaichi)*	*10*
Black cardamom *(bari elaichi)*	*2*
Cinnamon *(daalchini)* sticks	*2*
Cloves *(laung)*	*5*
Nutmeg *(Jaiphal)*	*1*
Ginger-garlic paste *(page 13)*	*20 gms / 4 tsp*
Red chilli powder	*5 gms / 1 tsp*
Turmeric *(haldi)* powder	*5 gms / 1 tsp*
Salt	*10 gm / 2 tsp*
Onion paste *(page 13)*	*200 gms / 1 cup*
Brown onion paste *(page 13)*	*50 gms / 3⅔ tbs*

For the curry:

Nihari Masala	
Har /Baheda/Amla *(trifla)*	
Dry ginger powder *(sonth)*	
Fennel *(saunf)* seeds	*5 gms / 1 tsp*
Cumin *(jeera)* seeds	
Coconut	
Garam masala *(page 13)*	*5 gms / 1 tsp*
Tomato purée, fresh *(page 13)*	*150 gms / ⅗ cup*
Water	*600 ml / 3 cup*
Khoya, grated *(page 13)*	*15 gms / 1 tbs*
Chickpea powder, roasted	*80 gms / 5⅓ tbs*
Saffron *(kesar)*	*a few strands*

Method:

1. Wash, clean and dry the lamb pieces.

2. Heat oil in a pan, add green cardamom, black cardomon, cinnamon, cloves and nutmeg. When they crackle, stir in the ginger-garlic paste, red chilli powder, turmeric powder and salt, stir fry for 4-5 minutes.

3. Add onion paste and cook on low heat stirring constantly. Sprinkle a little water as and when required. Cover and cook for 15-20 minutes.

4. Stir in the brown onion paste, nihari masala and garam masala, stir-fry till the oil seperates.

5. Add water, khoya and chickpea powder.

6. Add the lamb pieces along with saffron, cover and cook on very low heat for 25-30 minutes or till the lamb pieces are tender and the curry thickens.

7. Remove from heat, transfer to a serving bowl and serve hot.

VEGETARIAN

Clockwise from left: Gobhi Mussallam (page 59), Dhokla (page 61),
Hara Kabab and Daal Kabab (page 65) and Baida Kabab (page 63).

Paneer Akbari

Stuffed home made cheese chunks in a creamy tomato curry

Serves: 4, Preparation time: 20 minutes, Cooking time: 35 minutes

Ingredients:

Cottage cheese *(paneer*)* .... *600 gms*

For the Filling:
Khoya *(page 13)* .... *20 gms / 4 tsp*
Cottage cheese* *(paneer)*, mashed .... *30 gms / 2 tbs*
Cashewnuts, chopped .... *10 gms / 2 tsp*
Pickle masala (any) .... *5 gms / 1 tsp*
Tomato purée, thick *(page 13)* .... *20 gms / 4 tsp*

For the Batter:
Cornflour .... *50 gms / 3¹/3 tbs*
Salt .... *3 gms / ½ tsp*
Yellow colour .... *a pinch*
Water as required

For the Curry:
Oil .... *10 ml / 2 tsp + for frying*
Ginger-garlic paste *(page 13)* .... *10 gms / 2 tsp*
Tomato purée, fresh *(page 13)* .... *500 gms / 2 ½ cups*
Salt .... *5 gms / 1 tsp*
Red chilli powder .... *3 gms / ½ tsp*
White pepper powder .... *a pinch*
Fenugreek *(methi)* powder .... *a pinch*
Garam masala *(page 13)* .... *10 gms / 2 tsp*
Butter .... *10 gms / 2 tsp*
Cream .... *20 gms / 4 tsp*

Method:

For recipe of *paneer* turn to page 13.
1. Cut the paneer into 16 fingers and keep aside.
2. For the filling, mix together khoya, cottage cheese, cashewnuts, pickle masala and tomato purée.
3. Stuff the filling between two cottage cheese fingers.
4. For the batter, mix together cornflour, salt, yellow colour and water.
5. Dip the cottage cheese sandwich in the batter and deep fry in hot oil for 2-3 minutes. Remove, drain excess

oil and keep aside.
6. Heat oil (10 ml) in a pan and sauté ginger-garlic paste for 2-3 minutes. Add tomato purée and cook for 8-10 minutes till it thickens.
7. Add the seasoning and spices. Cook for 3-5 minutes, stir in the butter and cream. Remove from heat.
8. Arrange the fried cottage cheese sandwich on a dish and pour the curry on top.
9. Garnish with cream and serve hot.

Rogani Mushrooms

Mushrooms cooked in a rich onion and tomato curry

Serves: 4, Preparation time: 40 minutes, Cooking time: 30 minutes

Ingredients:

Mushrooms, without stems, boiled .... *600 gms*
Oil .... *100 ml / ½ cup*
Bayleaves *(tej patta)* *4*
Mace *(javitri)* .... *2 gms / ¹/3 tsp*
Cloves *(laung)* *4*
Green cardamom *(choti elaichi)* *4*
Black cardamom *(bari elaichi)* *4*
Cinnamon *(daalchini)* sticks, small *2*
Ginger-garlic paste *(page 13)* .... *20 gms / 4 tsp*
Tomato purée, fresh *(page 13)* .... *300 gms / 1½ cups*
Salt to taste

Red chilli powder .... *10 gms / 2 tsp*
Turmeric *(haldi)* powder .... *5 gms / 1 tsp*
Coriander powder .... *10 gms / 2 tsp*
Brown onion paste *(page 13)* .... *150 gms / ³/4 cup*
Yoghurt, whisked .... *50 gms / 3¹/3 tbs*
Water .... *100 ml / ½ cup*
Garam masala *(page 13)* .... *a pinch*
Green coriander, chopped .... *5 gms / 1 tsp*
Ginger, julienned .... *5 gms / 1 tsp*
Green chillies, julienned .... *5 gms / 1 tsp*

Method:

1. Heat oil in a handi *(pot)*, add bayleaves, mace, cloves, green cardamom, black cardamom and cinnamom, sauté till they crackle.
2. Stir in ginger-garlic paste dissolved in a little water and stir-fry till the water dries out.
3. Add tomato purée, salt, red chilli powder, turmeric powder, coriander powder and sauté for 2-3 minutes till the oil seperates.

4. Add the brown onion paste and yoghurt, stir-fry for 2-3 minutes, add the mushrooms alongwith water. Cook on low heat until the curry thickens and the mushrooms are cooked. Remove from heat and transfer to a serving dish.
5. Serve hot, garnished with garam masala, green coriander, julienned ginger and green chillies. (Picture on page 54).

Gucchi Paneer Keema

A delicacy of black mushrooms and cottage cheese stir-fried

Serves: 4, Preparation time: 20 minutes, Cooking time: 20-25 minutes

Ingredients:

Black mushrooms *(Gucchi)* .... 50 gms / 3 $^{1/3}$ tbs	Tomatoes, chopped .... 60 gms / 4 tbs
Cottage cheese* *(paneer)* cut to cubes 500 gms/2 ½ cups	Salt to taste
Oil .... 40 ml / 2 $^{2/3}$ tbs	Red chilli powder .... 4 gms / $^{3/4}$ tsp
Cumin *(jeera)* seeds .... 4 gms / $^{3/4}$ tsp	Turmeric *(haldi)* powder .... 2 gms / $^{1/3}$ tsp
Onions, chopped .... 35 gms / 2 $^{1/3}$ tbs	White pepper powder .... 2 gms / $^{1/3}$ tbs
Ginger, chopped .... 10 gms / 2 tsp	Green coriander, chopped .... 5 gms / 1 tsp
Green chillies, chopped .... 5 gms / 1 tsp	

Method:

*For receipe of *Paneer* turn to page 13.

1. Wash and soak the black mushrooms in water for 15 minutes. Drain and chop finely. Keep aside.

2. Heat oil in a pan, add cumin and sauté for a few seconds. Add onions and sauté till light brown, add ginger, green chillies, and tomatoes and stir-fry for 3-4 minutes.

3. Stir in seasoning and the remaining spices. Add the black mushrooms and cottage cheese. Cook on low heat until the cottage cheese and black mushrooms are completely done, stirring constantly. Remove from heat.

4. Transfer to a serving dish, garnish with chopped coriander and serve hot, accompanied by any Indian bread.

Gobhi Mussallam

Spiced whole cauliflower baked in an oven to keep the flavours alive

Serves: 4, Preparation time: 10-15 minutes, Cooking time: 30 minutes

Ingredients:

Cauliflower, floret only .... 175 gms	Salt to taste
Turmeric *(haldi)* powder .... a pinch	Garam masala *(page 13)* .... a pinch
Salt .... 10 gms / 2 tsp	Red chilli powder .... a pinch
Bayleaves *(tej patta)* 4	White pepper powder .... a pinch
Oil .... 30 ml / 2 tbs	Cashewnut paste .... 40 gms / 2 $^{2/3}$ tbs
Cloves *(laung)* 4	Yoghurt .... 40 gms / 2 $^{2/3}$ tbs
Green cardamom *(choti elaichi)* 4	Tomato purée, fresh *(page 13)* .... 50 gms / 3 $^{1/3}$ tbs
Ginger-garlic paste *(page 13)* .... 10 gms / 2 tsp	Brown onion paste *(page 13)* .... 50 gms / 3 $^{1/3}$ tbs
Water as required	Cream .... 50 gms / 3 $^{1/3}$ tbs
Butter .... 40 gms / 2 $^{2/3}$ tbs	

Method:

1. Wash and clean the cauliflower floret.

2. Boil water in a pan, add turmeric powder, salt and bayleaves. Gradually add the cauliflower to this brine solution. Cover cook on meduim heat till $^{3/4}$th done.

3. Remove from heat and drain excess water. Transfer the cauliflower to an oven proof dish.

4. Heat oil in a pan, add cloves and green cardamoms, sauté till they crackle. Stir in ginger-garlic dissolved in water (2 tsp). When the water dries out add butter, seasoning and spices.

5. Dissolve the cashewnut paste and yoghurt in water (½ cup) and add to the pan. Cook on low heat till it comes to a boil

6. Stir in the tomato purée and brown onion paste.

7. Cover and cook for about 5 minutes and stir in the cream.

8. Remove from heat and pour over the cauliflower floret.

9. Bake in a moderately hot oven for about 5-10 minutes. Remove from the oven, transfer to a serving dish and serve hot. (Picture on page 55).

Nadru Yakhani

Lotus stems cooked in a tangy yoghurt curry

Serves: 4, Preparation time: 20 minutes, Cooking time: 40 minutes

Ingredients:

Lotus stems .... 800 gms
Mustard oil.............................. 250 ml / 1 ¼ cups
Water as required
Cloves *(laung)*... 2
Green cardamom *(choti elaichi)* 2
Fennel *(saunf)* powder .... 30 gms / 2 tbs

Cinnamon *(daalchini)* powder .... 2 gms / ⅓ tsp
Cumin *(jeera)* powder .... 2 gms / ⅓ tsp
Salt to taste
Black cardamom *(bari elaichi)* powder ..... 6 gms / 1 tsp
Yoghurt, whisked .... 1 kg 500gms / 7 ½ cups

Method:

1. Scrape away the skin of the lotus stems. Cut into ½ " long pieces, discarding the ends pieces. Wash and drain.

2. Heat oil in a handi *(pot)* till it starts fuming and deep fry till the stems are half cooked. Remove, drain excess oil and keep aside.

3. Add water alongwith lotus stems in a handi *(pot)*, bring to a boil, add all the spices and stir.

4. Boil continuously on medium heat till the water is reduced to half. Stir in yoghurt, cover and cook further, stirring occasionally till the curry thickens and the lotus stems are tender.

5. Remove from heat, transfer to a serving dish and serve hot, accompanied by steamed rice.

Dhokla

A steamed savory preparation of gramflour

Serves: 4, Preparation time: 45 minutes, Cooking time: 30 minutes

Ingredients:

Gramflour *(besan)* .... 500 gms
Tartar powder .... 12 gms / 2 ⅓ tsp
Water.. 400 ml / 2 cups
Oil .... 40 ml / 2 ⅔ tbs
Vegetable soda .... 12 gms / 2 ⅓ tsp
Cumin *(jeera)* seeds................................ 10 gms / 2 tsp
Green chillies, chopped .... 10 gms / 2 tsp

Green coriander, chopped .... 50 gms / 3 ⅓ tbs
Coconut, grated .... 120 gms / ½ cup
Lemons 2
Ginger, chopped .... 10 gms / 2 tsp
Salt .... 20 gms / 4 tsp
Mustard *(raee)* seeds .... 20 gms / 4 tsp
Green chillies, slit.................................. 30 gms / 2 tbs

Method:

1. Dissolve tartar powder in water (50 ml).

2. Sieve gramflour in a bowl, add rest of the water to it and mix well to break all lumps. Add oil (1½ tbs), tartar dissloved in water and vegetable soda. Mix well.

3. Pour the gramflour mixture in a flat tray and steam for 15 minutes in a steamer or a double boiler with a lid on top. Remove and cool.

4. Make a fine paste by blending together the cumin seeds, green chillies, green coriander, coconut, juice of two lemons, ginger and salt. Keep aside.

5. Heat the remaining oil in a pan, add the mustard seeds and sauté till they crackle. Add slit green chillies, two cups of water. Bring to a boil and pour this over the cooked dhokla. Keep aside to soak.

6. Slice the dhokla into two portions. Apply the prepared paste evenly on one half and place the other half back on top.

7. Cut into square dices and serve. (Picture on page 55).

Khatte Baigan

Tangy Aubergines

Serves: 4, Preparation time: 30 minutes, Cooking time: 30 minutes

Ingredients:

Aubergine *(baigan)* .... 800 gms	Water, hot .... *400 ml / 2 cups*
Tamarind *(imlee)* .... 70 gms / 4 ²/₃ tbs	Salt to taste
Mustard oil .... 250 ml / 1 ¼ cup	Turmeric *(baldi)* powder .... *a pinch*
Cloves *(laung)* 2	Black cardamom *(bari elaichi)* powder .... 2 gms / ¹/₃ tsp
Green cardamom *(choti elaich)* 2	Fennel *(saunf)* powder .... 30 gms / 2 tbs
Green chillies, slit 4	Cinnamon *(daalchinni)* powder .... 2 gms / ¹/₃ tsp
Red chilli powder .... 20 gms / 4 tsp	Cumin *(jeera)* powder .... 2 gms / ¹/₃ tsp

Method:

1. Clean and cut the aubergines into quarters lengthwise.
2. Soak tamarind in sufficient water. Extract the tamarind juice and discard the seeds.
3. Heat mustard oil in a handi *(pot)* and fry the aubergines till half cooked. Remove, drain excess oil and keep aside.
4. Add cloves and green cardamom in the remaining oil and sauté till they crackle, add green chillies and sauté further for a minutes.

5. Stir in the red chilli powder, water (2 cups), salt, turmeric powder and the remaining spices. Bring to a boil and add the tamarind extract. Cook for 3-5 minutes till the curry begins to thicken.
6. Add the fried aubergines. Cover and cook on low heat till the curry has thickened and the aubergines are tender.
7. Remove from heat, transfer to a serving dish and serve hot, accompanied by a green salad and any Indian bread.

Baida Kabab

Skewered rolls of egg and potatoes, roasted in a charcoal grill

Serves: 4, Preparation time: 30-40 minutes, Cooking time: 10-15 minutes

Ingredients:

Eggs 11	Red chilli powder .... 2 gms / ¹/₃ tsp
Potatoes, boiled .... 200 gms	Ginger, chopped .... 10 gms / 2 tsp
Garam masala *(page 13)* .... 2 gms / ¹/₃ tsp	Green chillies, chopped .... 5 gms / 1 tsp
Chaat masala .... 2 gms / ¹/₃ tsp	Green coriander, chopped .... 5 gms / 1 tsp
Breadcrumbs .... 100 gms / ½ cup	Butter for basting .... 30 gms / 2 tbs
Salt .... 8 gms / 1 ½ tsp	

Method:

1. Boil 10 eggs, grate them and keep aside. Mash the boiled potatoes.
2. Mix together the grated eggs and mashed potatoes alongwith garam masala, chaat masala, bread crumbs, salt, red chilli powder, ginger, green chillies, green coriander and the raw egg.
3. Divide this mixture into 5 equal portions

4. Wrap each portion along the length of skewers using wet hands leaving a 2 cm gap between each. Roast for 5-10 minutes.
5. Remove and baste with butter. Roast further for 3-5 minutes or until cooked.
6. Remove from skewers and serve hot, accompanied by Mint chutney (page 91). (Picture on page 55).

Daal Panchmela

Mixed lentil curry

Serves: 4, Preparation time: 15 minutes, Cooking time: 1 hour

Ingredients:

Lentils *(malka masoor daal)* .... 40 *gms / 2 2/3 tbs*	Red chilli powder .... 5 *gms / 1 tsp*
Lentils *(chana daal)* .... 40 *gms / 2 2/3 tbs*	Oil ....35 *ml / 2 1/3 tbs*
Lentils *(dhuli urad daal)* .... 40 *gms / 2 2/3 tbs*	Butter .... 15 *gms / 1 tbs*
Lentils *(arhar daal)* .... 40 *gms / 2 2/3 tbs*	Cumin *(jeera)* seeds .... 5 *gms / 1 tsp*
Lentils *(dhuli moong daal)* .... 40 *gms / 2 2/3 tbs*	Ginger, chopped .... 10 *gms / 2 tsp*
Water as required	Tomatoes, chopped .... 60 *gms / 4 tbs*
Salt .... 10 *gms / 2 tsp*	Green coriander, chopped .... 5 *gms / 1 tsp*
Turmeric *(haldi)* powder .... 4 *gms / 3/4 tsp*	

Method:

1. Pick, clean and wash the lentils.

2. Put the lentils alongwith water, salt, turmeric powder and red chilli powder in a handi *(pot)* and cook on low heat for 40-45 minutes till the lentils are tender.

3. Remove from heat and keep aside.

4. Heat oil and butter in a pan, add cumin and sauté till they crackle. Add ginger, stir-fry to a light brown colour.

5. Add the tomatoes and sauté for a minute. Stir in the green coriander and remove from heat.

6. Temper the cooked lentils with this mixture and serve hot, accompanied by any Indian bread.

Hara Kabab

Shallow fried medallions of spinach and green peas

Serves: 4, Preparation time: 30 minutes, Cooking time: 20 minutes

Ingredients:

Peas, boiled .... 1 *kg*	Red chilli powder .... 3 *gms / 1/2 tsp*
Spinach *(palak)*, boiled .... 400 *gms / 2 cups*	Garam masala *(page 13)* ....3 *gms / 1/2 tsp*
Ginger, chopped .... 20 *gms / 4 tsp*	Chaat masala .... 5 *gms / 1 tsp*
Green chillies, chopped .... 10 *gms / 2 tsp*	Breadcrumbs, fresh .... 100 *gms / 1/2 cup*
Green coriander, chopped .... 10 *gms / 2 tsp*	Cornflour ....50 *gms / 3 1/3 tbs*
Salt to taste	Oil for frying

Method:

1. Mash the peas and blend the spinach without adding any water. Mix the mashed peas, spinach purée, ginger, green chillies, green coriander, salt, red chilli powder, garam masala, chaat masala, breadcrumbs and cornflour thoroughly.

2. Divide into equal portions and shape into medallions.

3. Heat oil in a kadhai *(wok)* to smoking point, deep fry the medallions a few at a time until crisp and golden brown on both sides. Remove and drain excess oil.

4. Arrange neatly on a serving platter and serve hot, accompanied by Coriander chutney (page 89). (Picture on page 55).

Daal Kabab

Spiced lentil cutlets

Serves: 4, Preparation time: 30 minutes, Cooking time: 15 minutes

Ingredients:

Lentils *(makla masoor daal)* .... 300 *gms*	Red chilli powder .... 2 *gms / 1/3 tsp*
Water as required	Chaat masala .... 4 *gms / 2/3 tsp*
Green chillies, chopped, deseeded .... 5 *gms / 1 tsp*	Breadcrumbs, fresh ....50 *gms / 3 2/3 tbs*
Green coriander, chopped .... 10 *gms / 2 tsp*	Cornflour .... 5 *gms / 1 tsp*
Ginger, finely chopped........................... 10 *gms / 2 tsp*	Garam masala *(page 13)* .... 2 *gms / 1/3 tsp*
Salt to taste	Oil for frying

Method:

1. Clean, wash and boil lentils alongwith water in a handi *(pot)* for 15 minutes. Drain and mash the lentils.

2. In a mixing bowl, add the mashed lentils alongwith green chillies, green coriander, ginger, salt, red chilli powder, chaat masala, bread crumbs, cornflour, garam masala and mix well.

3. Divide the mixture into 16 portions and shape into flat round cutlets. Heat oil in a kadhai *(wok)* and deep fry the cutlets, few at a time until crisp and light brown in colour. Remove and drain excess oil.

4. Serve hot, accompanied by Coriander chutney (page 89). (Picture on page 55).

Bhindi Kurkuri

Crunchy Okra

Serves: 4, Preparation time: 20 minutes, Cooking time: 20 minutes

Ingredients:

Okra *(bhindi)* .... *1 kg*	Chaat masala .... *3 gms / ½ tsp*
Salt to taste	Gramflour *(besan)* .... *45 gms / 3 tbs*
Red chilli powder .... *5 gms / 1 tsp*	Oil for frying
Garam masala *(page 13)* .... *5 gms / 1 tsp*	Ginger, julienned *(optional)* .... *7 gms / 1 ½ tsp*
Dry mango *(amchoor)* powder .... *3 gms / ½ tsp*	Green chillies, slit *(optional)* *2*

Method:

1. Snip off both ends of each okra, slice lengthwise into four slices.

2. Spread all sliced okra on a flat dish and sprinkle evenly with salt, red chilli powder, garam masala, mango powder and chaat masala. Mix well to coat okra evenly.

3. Sprinkle gramflour over the okra and mix in so they are coated evenly, preferably without adding any water.

4. Divide the okra into two portions.

5. Heat oil in a kadhai *(wok)* till it is smoking.

6. Fry one portion of the coated okra slices, seperating each lightly with a fork. Do not allow slices to stick to each other.

7. Remove from oil when both sides are crispy and brown in colour. Similarly, fry the other portion.

8. Remove to a serving platter and serve hot. Can be garnished with julienned ginger and slit green chillies.

Tilwale Aloo

Sesame seed coated potato cutlets

Serves: 4, Preparation time: 30 minutes, Cooking time: 25 minutes

Ingredients:

Potatoes, boiled .... *1 kg*	Ginger, finely chopped .... *8 gms / 1½ tsp*
Red chilli powder .... *4 gms / ^{2}/3 tsp*	Breadcrumbs, fresh .... *50 gms / 3 ^{1}/3 tsp*
Salt to taste	Cornflour .... *10 gms / 2 tsp*
Garam masala *(page 13)* .... *2 gms / ^{1}/3 tsp*	Sesame *(til)* seeds .... *75 gms / 5 tbs*
Green coriander, chopped .... *10 gms / 2 tsp*	Oil for frying
Green chillies, chopped .... *4 gms / ^{3}/4 tsp*	

Method:

1. Peel and mash the boiled potatoes.

2. In a mixing bowl, add the mashed potatoes alongwith red chilli powder, salt, garam masala, green coriander, green chillies, ginger, bread crumbs, cornflour and mix thoroughly.

3. Divide this mixture into 16 equal portions and shape into flat round cutlets.

4. Coat each cutlet with sesame seeds and deep fry in hot oil till crisp and golden brown in colour. Remove and drain excess oil.

5. Serve hot, accompanied by Mint chutney (page 91). (Picture on page 8).

Lauki Nazakat

Richly stuffed bottle gourd with an exotic curry

Serves: 4, Preparation time: 1 hour, Cooking time: 25-30 minutes

Ingredients:

Bottle gourd *(lauki)*	1 / 650 gms
Khoya *(page 13)*	50 gms / 3 ⅓ tbs
Cottage cheese* *(paneer)*	200 gms / 1 cup
Cashewnuts, chopped	40 gms / 2 ⅔ tbs
Melon *(magaz)* seeds	30 gms / 2 tbs
Raisins	25 gms / 5 tsp
Salt to taste	
Red chilli powder	3 gms / ½ tsp
Garam masala *(page 13)*	2 gms / ⅓ tsp
Dough for sealing	
Oil for frying	

For the curry:

Oil	50 gms / 3 ⅓ tbs
Cloves *(laung)*	4
Green cardamom *(choti elaichi)*	4

Black cardamom *(bari elaichi)*	4
Cinnamon *(daalchini)* sticks	2
Bayleaves *(tej patta)*	4
Ginger-garlic paste *(page 13)*	100 gms / ½ cup
Cashewnut paste	100 gms / ½ cup
Yoghurt	125 gms / ⅓ cup
Brown onion paste *(page 13)*	80 gms / 5 ⅓ tbs
Tomato purée, fresh	180 gms / 1 cup
Salt to taste	
Coriander powder	12 gms / 2 ⅓ tsp
Red chilli powder	5 gms / 1 tsp
White pepper powder	2 gms / ⅓ tsp
Cream	100 gms / ½ cup
Vetivier *(kewda)* essence	2-3 drops

Method:

For recipe of *Paneer,* turn to page 13.

1. Wash, peel and cut the ends of the bottle gourd to make a hollow tube.

2. For the filling, mix khoya and cottage cheese alongwith cashewnuts, melon seeds, raisins, salt to taste, red chilli powder and garam masala.

3. Stuff the bottle gourd with the prepared filling and seal both ends with dough.

4. Heat oil in a kadhai *(wok)* and deep fry the bottlegourd. Do not allow colour to change. Remove, drain excess oil and keep aside.

5. For the curry, heat oil in a heavy bottomed pan, add cloves, green cardamom, black cardamom, cinnamon and bay leaves, sauté till they crackle.

6. Stir in the ginger-garlic paste dissolved in a little water and stir-fry for a minute.

7. Mix the cashewnut paste in yoghurt and add to the pan. Cook for 5-10 minutes.

8. Add brown onion paste, tomato purée, salt, coriander powder, red chilli powder and white pepper powder. Cover and cook on low heat, stirring continuously till the curry thickens.

9. Stir in cream and vetivier. Remove from heat and discard the bayleaves.

10. Cut the prepared bottlegourd into 1½ inch thick slices and arrange neatly on a serving dish slightly overlapping each other and pour the curry on top.

11. Serve immediately, accompanied by any Indian bread.

Gulgule ki Chaat

Creamed lentil dumplings served with grated radish and spicy green chutney

Serves: 4, Preparation time: 1 hour 15 minutes, Cooking time: 30 minutes

Ingredients:

Lentils *(dhuli moong daal)*	200 gms / 1 cup
Lentils *(dhuli urad daal)*	50 gms / 3 ⅓ tbs
Water	125 ml / ⅓ cup
Oil for frying	

For the Chutney:

Coriander leaves	200 gms / 1 cup
Mint leaves	50 gms / 3 ⅓ tbs
Ginger, chopped	30 gms / 2 tbs

Green chillies	30 gms / 2 tbs
Lemon	4
Cumin *(jeera)* seeds, powdered	2 gms / ⅓ tsp
Salt to taste	
Water as required	
Onions rings	60 gms / 4 tbs
White radish, grated	120 gms / 1/2 cup
Radish leaves, chopped	40 gms / 2 ⅔ tbs

Method:

1. Soak the lentils for 1 hour. Drain and blend into a smooth paste using water.

2. With the prepared paste make lemon sized dumplings and keep aside.

3. Heat oil in a kadhai *(wok)* and deep fry the dumplings a few at a time till crisp and golden brown. Remove, drain excess oil and keep aside.

4. For the chutney, blend green coriander alongwith mint, ginger, green chillies, juice of 4 lemons, cumin powder, salt and water. Keep aside.

5. Place the dumplings neatly on a serving platter, pour the chutney on top and serve, garnished with onion rings, grated radish and radish leaves. (Picture on page 2).

Paneer Kofta in Spinach Curry

Soft cottage cheese dumplings in a flavourful spinach curry

Serves: 4, Preparation time: 10 minutes, Cooking time: 35 minutes

Ingredients:

Cottage cheese* (paneer), mashed .... 500 gms
Potatoes, boiled, mashed..................... 250 gms / 1 1/3 tsp
Cornflour .... 50 gms / 3 1/3 tbs
Salt .... 4 gms / 1/3 tsp
White pepper powder .... 3 gms / 1/2 tsp
Oil for frying
For the curry:
Spinach (palak) .... 1 kg
Oil .... 50 ml / 3 1/3 tbs

Garlic, chopped... 5 gms / 1 tsp
Tomato purée (page 13) .... 100 gms / 1/2 cup
Red chilli powder .... 3 gms / 1/2 tsp
Turmeric (haldi) powder .... 3 gms / 1/2 tsp
Coriander powder .... 3 gms / 1/2 tsp
Salt .... 5 gms / 1 tsp
Water .... 600 ml / 3 cup
Garam masala (page 13) .... 2 gms / 1/3 tsp

Method:

*For recipe of *paneer* turn to page 13.

1. Mix together the mashed cottage cheese and potatoes alongwith cornflour, salt and white pepper powder. Divide the mixture into 16 even sized balls.

2. Heat oil in a kadhai (wok) and deep fry the balls a few at a time until golden brown. Remove and keep aside.

3. Boil the spinach and blend to a purée.

4. Heat oil in a handi (pot), add garlic, spinach purée and cook for about 2-3 minutes. Stir in the tomato purée and mix well.

5. Add red chilli powder, turmeric powder, coriander powder and salt. Cook for 4-5 minutes.

6. Add water and bring to a boil. Add the fried cottage cheese balls, reduce heat and allow to simmer for 5-7 minutes. Stir in garam masala and cook till the curry has reduced to half. Remove from heat.

7. Carefully remove the balls 'Koftas' and place on a serving dish, pour the curry on top and serve hot, accompanied by Naan (page 95).

Besan ka Chila

Gramflour pancakes with an assortment of toppings

Serves: 4, Preparation time: 30 minutes, Cooking time: 30 minutes

Ingredients:

Gramflour (besan) .... 150 gms
Cumin (jeera) seeds................................... 5 gms / 1 tsp
Turmeric (haldi) powder .... 5 gms / 1 tsp
Red chilli powder .... 5 gms / 1 tsp
Salt to taste
Green chillies, chopped .... 5 gms / 1 tsp

Green coriander, chopped .... 10 gms / 2 tsp
Water as required
Cottage cheese* (paneer)...................... 100 gms / 1/2 cup
Tomatoes, chopped .... 50 gms / 3 1/3 tbs
Onions, chopped .... 50 gms / 3 1/3 tbs
Oil

Method:

*For recipe of *paneer,* turn to page 13.

1. Mix gramflour, cumin seeds, turmeric powder, red chilli powder, salt, green chillies, green coriander and water to make a batter of spreading consistency.

2. Cut the cottage cheese into small cubes and mix with onions and tomatoes. Keep aside in a bowl.

3. Heat a flat pan, brush it with oil and spread batter to

make a pancake of 7" diameter, cook until crisp on both sides. Sprinkle a little oil to avoid from sticking to the pan.

4. Sprinkle some of the cottage cheese mixture on top and remove.

5. Repeat till all the mixture is used to make 16 pancakes.

6. Arrange neatly on a serving platter and serve hot, accompanied by Pickle or Coriander chutney (page 89).

DESSERTS

Clockwise from left: Imarti (page 81), Lavang Latika (page 83),
Chocolate Mousse (page 79) and Kulfi Falooda (page 81).

Malpua

Shallow fried pancakes, soaked in saffron flavoured sugar syrup

Serves: 4, Preparation time: 45 minutes, Cooking time: 20 minutes

Ingredients:

Toned milk .... *2 litres / 10 cups*
Khoya, grated *(page 13)* .... *50 gms / 3 1/3 tbs*
Flour.. *20 gms / 4 tsp*
Cornflour .... *25 gms / 5 tsp*
Green cardamom *(choti elaichi)* powder .. *3 gms / ½ tsp*
For the sugar syrup:
Water............................... *250 gms / 1 1/3 cups*

Sugar .... *500 gms / 2 ½ cups*
Vetivier *(kewda)* essence............................... *5 ml / 1 tsp*
Yellow colour .... *3 gms / ½ tsp*
Clarified butter *(ghee)* ....*for frying*
For garnishing:
Pistachios, chopped, blanched................. *20 gms / 4 tsp*
Saffron *(kesar)* .... *a few strands*

Method:

1. Boil milk in a kadhai *(wok)* till it reduces to ¼ .
2. Add khoya and reduce heat to low, stir continuously till the khoya is completely dissolved.
3. Remove from heat onto a mixing bowl and allow to cool. Add flour, cornflour, green cardamom powder and mix thoroughly to make a batter.
4. In a pan, boil water alongwith sugar and cook till it reaches a thread like consistency. Mix in vetivier and yellow colour.
5. Heat clarified butter *(ghee)* in a frying pan. Add one ladle of batter and fry on both sides till golden brown in colour. Remove, drain excess oil and immerse directly into the sugar syrup. Repeat the same process until all the batter is used up.
6. Allow the malpua's to soak in syrup for a few minutes.
7. Remove from the sugar syrup and fold the malpua's into half or triangles. Arrange neatly on a serving platter and serve hot, garnished with pistachios and saffron and accompanied by Rabari (page 77).

Shahi Tukda Nawabi

A royal dessert of slices of rich bread soaked in a thickened flavoured milk, richly garnished

Serves: 4, Preparation time: 15 minutes, Cooking time: 1 hour

Ingredients:

Milk .... *1 litre / 5 cups*
Green cardamom *(choti elaichi)* powder .. *2 gms / 1/3 tsp*
Saffron *(kesar)* .... *a few strands*
Sugar .... *100 gms / ½ cup*
Milk bread slices *8*
Clarified butter *(ghee)* .... *200 gms / 1 cup*

For the rabari
Milk .... *2 litres / 10 cups*
Sugar .... *100 gms / ½ cup*
Green cardamom *(choti elaichi)* powder .. *2 gms / 1/3 tsp*
Saffron *(kesar)* .... *a few strands*
Almonds, slivered..................................... *10 gms / 2 tsp*
Pistachios, slivered .... *10 gms / 2 tsp*
Saffron *(kesar)* .... *a few strands*

Method:

1. Heat milk in a thick bottomed pan and bring to a boil. Add the cardamom powder and saffron. Remove from heat and mix in the sugar. Keep aside.
2. Heat clarified butter *(ghee)* in a seperate pan and fry the bread slices lightly. Remove, drain excess clarified butter.
3. Dip the fried bread slices in the prepared milk to immerse completely. Allow to stand for 10-15 minutes.

4. For the rabari: Heat milk in a pan and cook till it reduces to 1/3. Stir in the sugar, cardamom powder and saffron. Remove from heat and keep aside to cool.
5. Carefully lift the bread slices from the milk and place on a serving platter. Pour the rabari on top, garnish with slivered almonds and pistachios and strands of saffron.
6. Serve chilled or at room temperature. (Picture on page 72).

Zauq-e-Shahi

Dumplings of khoya, dipped in sugar syrup

Serves: 4, Preparation time: 45 minutes, Cooking time: 15 minutes

Ingredients:

Khoya, grated *(page 13)* .... *100 gms / ½ cup*	Sugar .... *200 gms / 1 cup*
Chenna .... *20 gms / 4 tsp*	Clarified butter *(ghee)* for frying
Flour, seived .... *5 gms / 5 tsp*	Saffron *(kesar)* .... *a pinch*
Water .... *1 litre / 5 cups*	Pistachios, blanched, chopped .... *20 gms / 4 tsp*
For the sugar syrup:	Rabari *(recipe given below)*
Water .... *175 ml / ³/4 cup*	

Method:

1. Gently mix the khoya, chenna and flour into a soft smooth dough with a little water. Divide the dough into 20 equal portions. Shape into round balls and keep aside.

2. Heat water in a pan, add sugar and stir continuously till the sugar is completely dissolved to make a thin sugar syrup. Remove from heat and keep aside.

3. Heat clarified butter in a kadhai *(wok)* on a low heat.

Put all the balls and gently stir to fry evenly on all sides. When the balls rise to the surface increase heat to moderate and cook till dark brown in colour.

4. Remove, drain excess oil and immerse in the sugar syrup. Allow to soak till cool.

5. Spread a layer or rabari on a serving dish, arrange the 'kala jamuns' on top. Garnish with saffron and pistachios and serve cold or at room temperature.

Makhana ki Kheer

Popped lotus seeds cooked in simmering milk flavoured with saffron

Serves: 4, Preparation time: 15 minutes, Cooking time: 40 minutes

Ingredients:

Phool makhana *(popped lotus seeds)* .... *50 gms / 3¹/3 tbs*	Nutmeg *(jaiphal)* powder .... *a pinch*
Oil for frying	Sugar .... *100 gms / ½ cup*
Milk .... *1½ litres / 7 cups*	Pistachios, slivered .... *7 gms / 1¹/3 tsp*
Raisins .... *20 gms / 4 tsp*	Almonds, blanched, slivered .... *7 gms / 1¹/3 tsp*
Green cardamom *(choti elaichi)* powder .... *a pinch*	Cashewnuts, slivered .... *7 gms / 1¹/3 tsp*
Mace *(javitri)* powder .... *a pinch*	

Method:

1. Clean the popped lotus seeds 'makhanas' and keep aside.

2. Heat oil in a kadhai *(wok)* and deep fry the makhanas on medium heat till crisp and golden brown. Remove from heat and drain excess oil.

3. Crush the fried makhanas with a rolling pin.

4. Heat milk in a seperate kadhai *(wok)* and bring to a boil. Stir in the crushed makhanas, raisins, green

cardamom powder, mace powder and nutmeg powder.

5. Reduce heat and cook for about 20 minutes, stirring constantly till the milk reduces to ³/4th.

6. Stir in the sugar. Remove from heat and transfer to a serving bowl.

7. Serve hot, garnished with slivered pistachios, almonds and cashewnuts.

Rabari

Vetivier and saffron flavoured thickened milk

Serves: 4, Preparation time: 10 minutes, Cooking time: 35 minutes

Ingredients:

Milk .... *1½ litres / 7 cups*	Saffron *(kesar)* .... *a few strands*
Khoya, grated *(page 13)* .... *100 gms / ½ cup*	Pistachios, blanched, chopped .... *20 gms / 4 tsp*
Sugar .... *100 gms / ½ cup*	Vetivier *(kewda)* water .... *3-4 drops*
Green cardamom *(choti elaichi)* powder .... *a pinch*	

Method:

1. Heat milk in a kadhai *(wok)*, on moderate heat. Stir continuously till the milk reduces to ¹/5th.

2. Add khoya and cook on very low heat for 2-3 minutes, stirring continuously till the khoya is dissolved.

3. Add the sugar and cardamom powder and stir till sugar

is completely dissolved.

4. Remove from heat and transfer to a serving dish. Allow to cool and refrigerate.

5. Garnish with saffron, pictashios and vetivier and serve.

Badam Halwa

A rich almond delight served, garnished with saffron and pistachios

Serves: 4, Preparation time: 12 hours, Cooking time: 40 minutes

Ingredients:

Almonds .... 500 gm / 2½ cups	Sugar powder .... 125 gms / 3/4 cup
Clarified butter (ghee) .... 250 gms / 1 1/3 cups	Saffron (kesar) .... a few strands
Milk .... 150 ml / 3/4 cup	Pistachios, blanched, chopped .... 20 gms / 4 tsp

Method:

1. Soak almonds in water overnight. Peel the skin and dry. Blend coarsely without adding any water.
2. Heat oil in a kadhai (wok), add the powdered almonds, stir-fry on low heat till golden brown in colour.
3. Stir in the milk and sugar. When the milk comes to a boil, reduce heat and cook till the milk reduces to half.
4. Remove from heat and cover with a lid. Allow to rest for 5 minutes.
5. Remove onto a serving dish, garnish with saffron and pistachios and serve hot.

Chenna Payas

Rasgulla shaped rasmalai in a curd cheese flavoured rabari, one of the best Indian sweet meats

Serves: 4, Preparation time: 20 minutes, Cooking time: 45 minutes

Ingredients:

Milk .... 2 ½ litres / 12 ½ cups	Sugar .... 50 gms / 3 1/3 tbs
Or Chenna .... 350 gms / 1 3/4 cups	Green cardamom (choti elaichi) powder .. 2 gms / 1/3 tsp
Sugar .... 400 gms / 2 cups	Saffron (kesar) .... 2 gms / 1/3 tsp
Water .... 300 ml / 1½ cup	Almond, slivered .... 10 gms / 2 tsp
Flour (maida) .... 25 gms / 5 tsp	Pistachios, slivered .... 10 gms / 2 tsp
Milk .... 1 litre / 5 cups	Saffron (kesar) .... a few strands

Method:

1. Boil milk in a pan and curdle it by adding white vinegar or lemon juice.
2. Remove from heat, drain the whey and mash the curd cheese well. Seperate 300 gms for payas and 50 gms for the dumplings.
3. Prepare the sugar syrup by boiling together sugar and water till it reaches a thread like consistency. Reduce heat to low.
4. For the dumplings, make about 40 dumplings and simmer in sugar syrup till they swell upto double their size. (To aid in swelling, the simmering syrup should be allowed to froth which is possible by adding maida to it before adding the dumplings). Remove the dumplings from the sugar syrup and keep aside.
5. For the payas, cook the curd cheese seperated for the payas in a kadhai (wok) on very low heat. Add the sugar and stir continuously to prevent the payas from sticking to the sides. Cook till it begins to leave the sides. Remove from heat and allow to cool.
6. For the rabari, in a kadhai (wok), add milk and cook on medium heat till it reduces to 1/3, add the cardamom powder and saffron. Remove from heat and add sugar, stir till it dissolves completely.
7. Transfer the prepared rabari to the kadhai (wok) containing the payas and cook for about 10-12 minutes. Remove from heat and keep aside to cool.
8. Gently fold in the prepared 'rasgoolas' dumplings into the prepared payas and serve chilled, garnished with almonds, pistachios and saffron.

Chocolate Mousse

Melted chocolate in a fluffy and rich dessert

Serves: 4, Preparation time: 15 minutes, Cooking time: 15 minutes

Ingredients:

Chocolate slab .... 100 gms	Gelatine .... 20 gms /4 tsp
Cocoa powder .... 100 gms / ½ cup	Cornflour .... 40 gms / 2 2/3 cup
Sugar .... 100 gms / ½ cup	Water .... 500 ml / 2 ½ cups
Cream .... 120 ml / 3/4 cup	Egg, white only 2

Method:

1. Blend together the chocolate slab, cocoa powder, sugar, cream (4 tsp), gelatine, cornflour and water.
2. Cook on low heat till it reaches a sauce-like consistency.
3. Remove from heat and allow to cool. Pass through a muslin cloth and keep aside.
4. Blend in the balance cream and the egg whites. Pour into champagne glasses and keep in a refrigerator to allow to set.
5. Serve chilled with chocolate flakes. (Picture on page 73).

Kulfi

The Indian home made ice cream, very rich and flavourful

Serves: 4, Preparation time: 2 hours, Cooking time: 30 minutes

Ingredients:

Milk .... 1½ litres / 7 cups	Green cardamom (choti elaichi) powder .... a pinch
Saffron (kesar) .... a few strands	Pistachios, blanched .... 20 gms / 4 tsp
Yellow colour .... 2-3 drops	Cashewnuts, chopped .... 20 gms / 4 tsp
Sugar .... 100 gms / ½ cup	

Method:

1. Soak saffron in 1 tbs water.
2. Heat milk in a kadhai *(wok)*, add yellow colour and cook on medium heat stirring constantly for about 20 minutes till it reduces to ¼ th.
3. Remove the milk from heat and add sugar. Stir till the sugar is completely dissolved.
4. Add the remaining ingredients, mix well and pour the mixture into kulfi moulds.
5. Keep the moulds in a freezer for 1½ hours to allow to set.
6. Remove from the freezer, dip the bottom of the moulds in hot water for a few seconds. Invert onto a serving plate and serve immediately, accompanied by Falooda.

Falooda

Freshly prepared cornflour vermicelli served with kulfi

Serves: 4, Preparation time: 10 minutes, Cooking time: 15-20 minutes

Ingredients:

Water .... 400 ml / 2 cups	Yellow colour (optional) .... a few drops
Cornflour .... 100 gms / ½ cup	

Method:

1. Take water in a kadhai *(wok)*, add the cornflour and mix well. Stir in the yellow colour.
2. Cook on low heat stirring continuously till the mixture thickens and becomes gelatinous. Remove from heat.
3. Pour into a falooda press. Place the press over a container of cold water.
4. Press the mixture out in one continous stream without stopping.
5. Remove the falooda press. Change the cold water and store the falooda in a refrigerator and use as required.
6. If desired falooda can be flavoured with Roohafza/ Vetivier/Rose water.
7. Serve chilled, as an accompaniment to Kulfi.

Imarti

Lentil roundels cooked in clarified butter and seized in saffron flavoured sugar syrup

Serves: 4, Preparation time: 1 hour 15 minutes, Cooking time: 30-40 minutes

Ingredients:

Lentils (dhuli urad daal) .... 250 gms / 1¼ cups	**For the sugar syrup**
Water .... 500 ml / 2½ cups	Sugar .... 1 kg 250 gms / 6 1/4 cups
Refined flour .... 25 gms / 5 tsp	Water .... 1½ litre / 7 cups
Cornflour .... 25 gms / 5 tsp	Saffron (kesar) .... a few strands
Yellow colour .... 5 ml / 1 tsp	Vetivier (kewda) water .... 5 ml / 1 tsp
Clarified butter (ghee) .... 750 ml / 3 3/4 cups	

Method:

1. Wash and soak the lentils in water for 1 hour.
2. Drain the lentils and blend to a coarse paste 'peethi'. Add colour and keep aside.
3. Prepare the sugar syrup by boiling water alongwith sugar for about 20 minutes till it reaches a thread-like consistency. Stir in the saffron and vetivier. Reduce heat to low.
4. Heat the clarified butter in a flat kadhai *(wok)*.
5. Stuff the prepared paste into a cloth piping bag and pipe out the paste in the kadhai in circles and then overlapping with circles on the borders.
6. Fry for 2-3 minutes on each side until a golden yellow colour is achieved.
7. Remove and immerse directly into the hot sugar syrup. Allow to soak for for 2 minutes.
8. Remove, drain excess syrup and serve hot. (Picture on page 73).

Kujja Kulfi

This home made ice cream is set and served in special earthenware cups

Serves: 4, Preparation time: 2 hours, Cooking time: 30 minutes

Ingredients:

Milk .... *1 litre / 5 cups*	Green cardamom *(choti elaichi)* powder .... *a pinch*
Saffron *(kesar)* .... *a few strands*	Cashewnuts, chopped .... *20 gms / 4 tsp*
Sugar .... *65 gms / 4 ¹/₃ tsp*	Pistachios, blanched, chopped................. *15 gms / 1 tbs*
Yellow colour .... *2-3 drops*	

Method:

1. Soak the saffron in 1 tbs water.

2. Heat milk in a kadhai *(wok)* and cook on medium heat for about 20 minutes, stirring constantly till reduced to ¼ th.

3. Remove milk from heat and stir in the sugar till it is completely dissolved.

4. Mix in the soaked saffron, yellow colour, green cardamom powder and the nuts.

5. Fill into earthenware moulds 'kujja', cover with a lid and seal with dough.

6. Place the moulds in a freezer for 1½ hours to allow to set.

7. Remove from the freezer, remove the lid and serve immediately.

Lavang Latika

Clove flavoured stuffed and rolled pancakes deep fried and seized in syrup

Serves: 4, Preparation time: 1 hour, Cooking time: 30 minutes

Ingredients:

Refined flour............................. *200 gms / 1 cup*	Clove *(laung)* powder .... *3 gms / ½ tsp*
Saffron *(kesar)* .... *a few strands*	Sugar, powdered .... *30 gms / 2 tbs*
Water... *60 ml / 4 tbs*	Cloves *(laung)*... *12*
Veg.oil .... *30 ml / 2 tbs*	Oil for frying
For the filling:	**For the sugar syrup:**
Khoya, mashed *(page 13)* .... *125 gms / ³/₄ cup*	Sugar .... *500 gms / 2 ½ cups*
Almonds, slivered................................ *20 gms / 4 tsp*	Water.. *700 ml / 3 ½ cups*
Pistachios, slivered .... *20 gms / 4 tsp*	

Method:

1. Sieve the flour and make a well in the centre.

2. Soak saffron in 1 tbs water for 5 minutes and pour into the well alongwith vegetable oil and mix well.

3. Mix water from time to time and knead to make a hard dough. Cover with a wet cloth and allow to rest for 15 minutes.

4. For the filling, mix together khoya, almonds, pistachios, clove powder and sugar. Divide into 12 equal portions.

5. Boil sugar with water to prepare the sugar syrup.

6. Divide the dough into 12 equal portions and shape into balls. Roll out each of these balls into 6" diameter pancakes.

7. Place one portion of filling in the centre of each pancake and brush the edges with water.

8. Fold the pancakes from the right edge to the centre and press firmly to seal in the filling. Repeat from left edge to give a 2" wide strip.

9. Keeping the folded side out, make a ring with the strip. Brush the edges with water and press firmly to seal, secure with a clove.

10. Shallow fry on very low heat till crisp and golden brown in colour. Remove and drain excess oil.

11. Dip in hot sugar syrup to submerge completely, turning gently if required. Allow to soak for 2-3 minutes. Remove and drain excess syrup.

12. Arrange neatly on a serving platter and serve. (Picture on page 73).

ACCOMPANIMENTS

Clockwise from left: Dahi Bhalla (page 87), Papad, Prawn Biryani and Lamb Biryani (page 94) and Chilman Biryani (page 93).

Dahi Bhalla

Lentil dumplings in a tangy and spiced yoghurt, served with tamarind chutney
Serves: 4, Preparation time: 2 hours, Cooking time: 30 minutes

Ingredients:

For the bhallas:

Lentils *(dhuli urad daal)*	200 gms / 1 cup
Water	600 ml / 3 cups
Salt	2 gms / $1/3$ tsp
Cumin *(jeera)* seeds	5 gms / 1 tsp
Ginger, chopped	10 gms / 2 tsp
Green chillies, chopped	5 gms
Oil	250 ml / 1 $1/3$ cup

For the yoghurt mixture:

Yoghurt, thick, whisked	400 gms / 2 cups
Sugar	5 gms / 1 tsp
Salt	2 gms / $1/3$ tsp
Cumin *(jeera)* seeds, roasted pounded	4 gms / $3/4$ tsp
Black rock salt *(kala namak)*	2 gms / $1/3$ tsp
White pepper powder	2 gms / $1/3$ tsp

For garnishing:

Ginger, julienned	5 gms / 1 tsp
Green chillies, julienned	5 gms / 1 tsp
Green coriander, chopped	5 gms / 1 tsp
Red chilli powder	a pinch
Cumin *(jeera)* seeds, roasted, pounded	a pinch
Mint leaves	4 sprigs
Tamarind chutney	40 gms / 2 $2/3$ tbs

Method:

1. Clean the lentils and soak in water for 2 hours. Drain and grind to a fine paste adding a little water if required.
2. Remove onto a mixing bowl and add salt, cumin seeds, ginger, green chillies and mix well. Shape into even sized balls.
3. Heat oil in a kadhai *(wok)*, add the prepared balls, a few at a time using wet hands and deep fry till golden brown in colour. (Make a hole in the centre of the ball with the thumb just before frying). Remove, drain on paper towels.

4. Soak the prepared bhallas in sufficient luke warm water till they are soft.
5. To the whisked yoghurt add sugar, salt, cumin powder, black rock salt and white pepper powder. Mix well.
6. Remove the bhallas from water, squeeze out excess water and add to the yoghurt. Keep aside for 10-15 minutes.
7. Serve chilled, garnished with ginger, green chillies, green coriander, red chilli powder, cumin powder, mint leaves and tamarind chutney.

Kashmiri Mooli ka Raita

A favourite among Kashmiris, grated radish in yoghurt
Serves: 4, Preparation time: 20 minutes

Ingredients:

White radish, grated	350 / 1 $3/4$ cup
Yoghurt, thick	600 gms / 3 cups
Salt	8 gms / 1½ tsp
Green chillies, chopped	8 gms / 1½ tsp
Walnuts, chopped	50 gms / 3 $1/3$ tbs

Method:

1. Place the grated radish in a muslin cloth and squeeze out excess water. Remove and keep aside.
2. In a mixing bowl, whisk yoghurt alongwith salt. Add the grated radish, green chillies and walnuts and mix well.
3. Remove onto a serving dish and serve chilled, as an accompaniment to a meal. (Picture overleaf).

Bhindi Raita

Fried okra in yoghurt
Serves: 4, Preparation time: 15 minutes

Ingredients:

Okra *(bhindi)*	100 gms / ½ cup
Oil for frying	
Yoghurt, thick	900 gms / 4 ½ cups
Salt to taste	
Red chilli powder	a pinch
Cumin *(jeera)* seeds, roasted, powdered	a pinch

Method:

1. Wash, clean and dry the okra. Slice them diagonally (2 mm) thick.
2. Deep fry in oil till crisp. Remove and drain excess oil.
3. Whisk yoghurt alongwith salt to taste. Add the fried okra and mix well.
4. Garnish with red chilli powder and cumin powder. Serve chilled, as an accompaniment to a dish. (Picture overleaf).

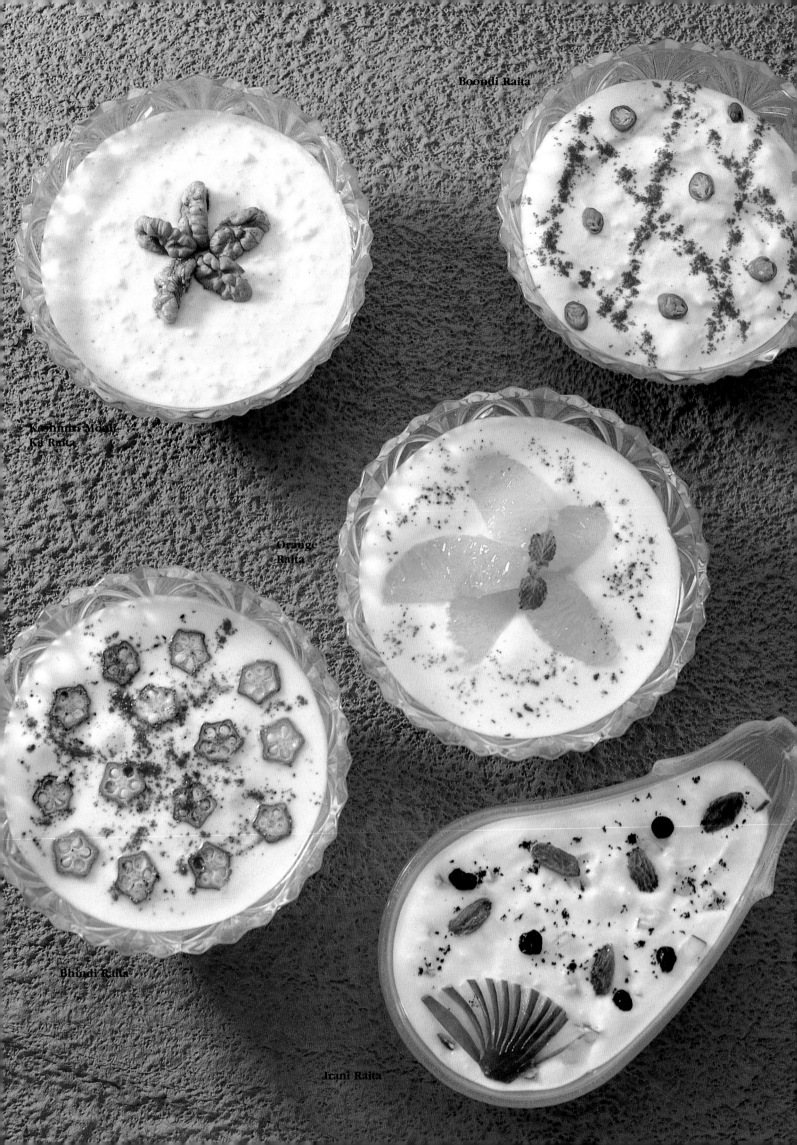

Boondi Raita

Kashmiri Mooli
Ka Raita

Orange
Raita

Bhindi Raita

Irani Raita

Boondi Raita

Crisp small dumplings of gramflour in yoghurt

Serves: 4, Preparation time: 30-40 minutes

Ingredients:

Gramflour *(besan)* .... *40 gms / 2½ tbs*	Oil for frying
Salt to taste	Yoghurt, thick .... *925 gms / 4½ cups*
Baking powder .... *2 gms / ⅓ tsp*	Cumin *(jeera)* seeds, roasted, crushed .... *a pinch*
Water as required	Red chilli powder .... *2 gms / ⅓ tsp*

Method:

1. For the Boondi: Mix together the gramflour, salt (¼ tsp) and baking powder in a bowl, gradually add water and whisk to a smooth batter, having consistancy of heavy cream.

2. Heat oil in a deep-frying pan. Pour about 2 tbs of batter at a time into a frying spoon with several holes. Hold the spoon above the pan and press the batter through the holes with your fingers. They will froth in the hot oil, then rise to the surface.

3. Fry until crisp and golden in colour. Remove on paper towels to drain. Repeat the process for all the batter.

4. In a bowl of warm water, put 2-3 tbs of boondis, leave to soften, then gently squeeze between palms to remove excess water, keep aside.

5. Whisk yoghurt alongwith salt to taste, cumin seeds, red chilli powder in a bowl until smooth and creamy.

6. Stir in the soaked boondi and serve at room temperature or chilled, as an accompaniment to any meal.

Orange Raita

Whisked yoghurt served with fresh oranges

Serves: 4, Preparation time: 15 minutes

Ingredients:

Yoghurt, thick .... *925 gms / 4½ cups*	Oranges .... *200 gms / 1 cup*
Salt to taste	Cumin *(jeera)* seeds, roasted, pounded .... *a pinch*

Method:

1. Whisk yoghurt and salt together.

2. Peel, clean and seperate the oranges into segments, cut

into 10 mm squares and add to the yoghurt.

3. Chill and serve, garnished with cumin powder.

Irani Raita

Whisked yoghurt with raisins and honey

Serves: 4, Preparation time: 15 minutes

Ingredients:

Cucumber .... *450 gms*	White pepper powder .... *3 gms / ½ tsp*
Yoghurt, whisked .... *800 gms / 4 cups*	Salt to taste
Honey .... *80 gms / 5⅓ tbs*	Cumin *(jeera)* seeds, roasted, powdered .. *3 gms / ½ tsp*
Raisins, chopped .... *40 gms / 2⅔ tbs*	Green Coriander, chopped .... *5 gms / 1 tsp*

Method:

1. Peel and chop the cucumbers finely.

2. To the whisked yoghurt add honey, raisins, cucumber, white pepper powder and salt. Mix well.

3. Transfer to a serving bowl and sprinkle cumin powder

and garnish with green coriander.

4. Serve chilled or at room temperature, as an accompaniment to a meal.

Coriander Chutney

A delightful blend of fresh coriander, a must with all kababs

Serves: 4, Preparation time: 20 minutes

Ingredients:

Green coriander, chopped .... *200 gms / 1 cup*	Lemon *1*
Mint leaves, chopped .... *50 gms / 3⅓ tbs*	Cumin *(jeera)* seeds, pounded .... *3 gms / ½ tsp*
Ginger, chopped .... *30 gms / 2 tbs*	Salt to taste
Green chillies, deseeded, chopped *6*	Water as required

Method:

1. Wash the green coriander and mint leaves thoroughly.

2. Blend green coriander leaves alongwith all the

ingredients to a smooth paste. Transfer onto a serving bowl and serve, as an accompaniment to any dish.

Radish & Walnut
Chutney

Saunth

Tomato
Chutney

Mint
Chutney

Yellow Chutni

Coriander
Chutney

Coconut
Chutney

Coconut Chutney

Freshly grated coconut chutney flavoured with mustard

Serves: 4, Preparation time: 15 minutes

Ingredients:

Coconut, shelled, grated .... *320 gms / 1½ cups*	Lemon .... *½*
Green chillies .... *12 gms / 1¹/₃ tsp*	**For the tempering:**
Ginger, peeled... *12 gms / 1¹/₃ tsp*	Oil .... *10 ml / 2 tsp*
Lentils *(chana daal)*, roasted .... *40 gms*	Lentils *(urad daal)*, washed .... *5 gms / 1 tsp*
Water.. *200 ml / 1 cup*	Mustard *(raee)* seeds .... *4 gms / ³/₄ tsp*
Salt to taste	Red chillies, whole *2*

Method:

1. Cut the green chillies and ginger into small pieces. Blend into a smooth paste alongwith coconut, lentils and water. Remove to a bowl.
2. Add salt and juice of half a lemon.

3. Heat oil in a pan, add the lentils, mustard seeds and red chillies, sauté till they crackle. Pour the tempering over the chutney and serve cold, as an accompaniment to any dish.

Mint Chutney

Garden fresh mint paste with yoghurt and spices

Serves: 4, Preparation time: 20 minutes

Ingredients:

Mint, chopped .... *100 gms / ½ cup*	Water.. *20 ml / 4 tsp*
Green coriander, chopped .... *100 gms / ½ cup*	Yoghurt.. *60 gms / 4 tbs*
Cumin *(jeera)* seeds .... *5 gms / 1 tsp*	Dry pomegranate *(anardana)* powder .... *30 gms / 2 tbs*
Ginger, finely chopped............................ *25 gms / 5 tsp*	Salt to taste
Green chillies, finely chopped .... *25 gms / 5 tsp*	Lemon *1*

Method:

1. Wash the green coriander and mint leaves thoroughly.
2. Blend the mint leaves and green coriander alongwith and all the other ingredients except salt and lemon.

3. Transfer to a serving bowl and mix in salt to taste and juice of a lemon. Serve, as an accompaniment to any dish.

Tomato Chutney

Spicy and tangy tomato dip, best savoured with vegetarian snacks

Serves: 4, Preparation time: 10 minutes, Cooking time: 5 minutes

Ingredients:

Tomatoes ....*335 gms / 1³/₄ cup*	Oil .... *10 gms / 2 tsp*
Ginger, chopped .... *8 gms / 1½ tsp*	Lentils *(urad daal)*, washed .... *5 gms / 1 tsp*
Red chilli powder.................................... *2 gms / ¹/₃ tsp*	Red chillies, whole *1*
Coconut, shelled .... *28 gms / 5 tsp*	Mustard *(raee)* seeds .... *4 gms / ³/₄ tsp*

Method:

1. Blanch the tomatoes by putting in boiling water for a minute. Remove and allow to cool.
2. Blend together the tomatoes, ginger, red chilli powder and coconut to make a purée. Transfer to a serving bowl.

3. Heat oil in a pan, add the lentils, red chillies and mustard seeds, sauté till they crackle.
4. Pour this tempering over the prepared chutney and serve as an accompaniment to any dish.

Yellow Chutney

Roasted gramflour and spices blended together with a distinctive flavour of red chillies and mustard

Serves: 4, Preparation time: 15 minutes

Ingredients:

Black gram *(chana)* .... *200 gms / 1 cup*	Mustard *(raee)* seeds .... *2 gms / ¹/₃ tsp*
Water... *100 ml / ½ cup*	Curry leaves .... *1 sprig*
Salt to taste	Red chillies, whole *5*
Oil .... *10 ml / 2 tsp*	

Method:

1. Blend black gram with water into a smooth paste. Transfer to a bowl, add salt and mix well.
2. Heat oil in a pan, add mustard seeds and sauté till they

crackle. Add curry leaves and red chillies. Stir and remove from heat. Pour the prepared tempering over the chutney and serve as an accompaniment to any dish.

Chilman Biryani

Lamb biryani cooked on low heat, covered with a rich puff
Serves: 4, Preparation time: 30 minutes, Cooking time: 1 hour 45 minutes

Ingredients:

Lamb, cut into pieces	500 gms
Basmati rice,	500 gms / 2½ cups
Water as required	
Mace *(javitri)* powder	2 gms / ⅓ tsp
Green cardamom *(choti elaichi)*	4
Black cardamom *(bari elaichi)*	4
Cloves *(laung)*	4
Bayleaves *(tej patta)*	5
Oil	200 ml / 1 cup
Onions, sliced	50 gms / 3⅓ tbs
Ginger-garlic paste *(page 13)*	25 gms / 5 tsp
Salt	10 gms / 2 tsp
Red chilli powder	10 gms / 2 tsp
Water	1 litre / 5 cups
Brown onion paste *(page 13)*	50 gms / 3⅓ tbs
Saffron *(kesar)*	a few strands
Vetivier *(kewda)* water	10 ml / 2 tsp
Onions, sliced, browned	60 gms / 4 tbs

For the Chilman (*puff*) covering:

Flour	100 gms / ½ cup
Butter	100 gms / ½ cup
Water	75 ml / 5 tbs

Method:

1. Wash and soak rice in water for 1 hour. Drain and boil in sufficient water alongwith whole spices till ¾ done. Remove from heat, drain and keep aside.
2. Heat oil in a pan, add onion, fry until brown, add ginger-garlic paste with lamb pieces and stir-fry for about 8-10 minutes. Add salt, red chilli powder and water and cook for about 20-25 minutes on medium heat.
3. Stir in the brown onion paste and cook till lamb pieces are tender and the curry thickens. Remove from heat.

4. For the 'chilman' puff covering, mix butter into the flour, add water and knead to a smooth soft dough.
5. In an oven proof handi *(pot)* place alternate layers of rice and lamb curry. Sprinkle saffron, vetvier and onions, browned. Seal the handi *(pot)* with prepared the puff covering and place in a moderately hot oven (150°C-175°C) for 20 minutes or till the covering is cooked.
6. Remove and serve hot, accompanied by Kashmiri Mooli ka Raita (page 87).

Chicken Biryani

Chicken and rice cooked in a flavourful stock, finished on dum
Serves: 4, Preparation time: 1 hour, Cooking time: 1 hour

Ingredients:

Chicken, cut into pieces	880 gms
Basmati rice	800 gms
Oil	110 ml / ½ cup
Ginger-garlic paste *(page 13)*	10 gms / 2 tsp
Water	100 ml / ½ cup
Salt	6 gms / 1⅓ tsp
Green cardamom *(choti elaichi)*	8
Black cardamom *(bari elaichi)*	8
Cloves *(laung)*	8
Cinnamon *(daalchini)* sticks	2
Black peppercorns	1 gm
Bayleaves *(tej patta)*	4
Onion, chopped	130 gms / 1⅓ cups
Green chillies, chopped	10 gms / 2 tsp
Yoghurt	100 gms / ½ cup
Chicken stock	30 ml / 1½ cups

Method:

1. Clean, wash and soak the rice for 1 hour.
2. Heat oil (10 ml) in a pan, add chicken pieces, ginger-garlic paste, water and salt (2 gms). Cover and cook on low heat till all the water dries. Remove the chicken pieces and keep aside.
3. Heat oil (100 ml) in a handi *(pot)*, add the whole spices. Sauté till they crackle, add the onions and stir-fry till light brown in colour.
4. Add green chillies and chicken pieces, sauté for a

minutes. Stir in yoghurt, chicken stock and remaining salt. Bring to a boil, stirring continously and reduce heat.
5. Add the drained rice to the pot and stir from time to time till stock has reduced to the level of rice. Cover with a wet cloth.
6. Cook on very low heat (dum) until the rice is cooked and the chicken pieces are tender.
7. Remove from heat, transfer to a serving platter and serve hot, accompanied by Irani raita (page 89).

Saunth

A sweet and tangy concoction of tamarind pulp and spices.
Serves: 4, Preparation time: 15 minutes

Ingredients:

Dry ginger *(sonth)* powder	4 gms / ¾ tsp
Sugar	250 gms / 1⅓ cup
Dry mango *(amchoor)* powder	100 gms / ½ cup
White pepper powder	5 gms / 1 tsp
Red chilli powder	10 gms / 2 tsp
Black rock salt *(kala namak)*	5 gms / 1 tsp
Garam masala *(page 13)*	2 gms / ⅓ tsp
Cumin *(jeera)* powder	2 gms / ⅓ tsp
Fennel *(saunf)* powder	2 gms / ⅓ tsp
Water	175 ml / ¾ cups

Method:

1. Mix together all the ingredients to a smooth paste. Take care to see that no lumps are formed.

2. Strain through a strainer and transfer to a serving dish.
3. Serve cold, as an accompaniment to any dish.

Lamb Biryani

Tender lamb cooked with rice and traditional spices

Serves: 4, Preparation time: 30 minutes, Cooking time: 1 hour 30 minutes

Ingredients:

Lamb, cut into pieces .... *500 gms*	Onions, chopped .... *50 gms / 3¹/₃ tbs*
Basmati rice .... *500 gms / 2½ cups*	Ginger-garlic paste *(page 13)* .... *25 gms / 5 tsps*
Water... *l litre / 5 cups*	Onion paste, browned *(page 13)* .... *50 gms / 3¹/₃ tbs*
Mace *(jaiphal)* .... *2 gms / ¹/₃ tsp*	Red chilli powder.................................... *10 gms / 2 tsp*
Black cardamom *(bari elaichi)* .... *2 gms / ¹/₃ tsp*	Salt .... *10 gms / 2 tsp*
Green cardamom *(choti elaichi)*............... *2 gms / ¹/₃ tsp*	Saffron *(kesar)* .... *a few strands*
Cloves *(laung)*... *2 gms / ¹/₃ tsp*	Vetivier *(kewda)* essence .... *a few drops*
Bayleaves *(tej patta)* 5	Onions, chopped, browned .... *50 gms / 3¹/₃ tbs*
Oil .... *200 ml / 1 cup*	

Method:

1. Clean, wash and soak the rice for 30 minutes. Drain and keep aside.

2. Heat water (750 ml / 3½ cups) in a pot till it comes to a boil, add the rice, mace, black and green cardamoms, cloves and bayleaves. Cover and cook till the rice is ³/₄ th done. Remove from heat and keep aside.

3. Heat oil in a pan, and the onions and sauté till light brown in colour. Add the ginger-garlic paste and sauté for a minute.

4. Add the lamb pieces and stir-fry for 10 minutes. Stir in the salt, red chilli powder and water (300 ml / 1½ cups)

cover and cook for 20 - 25 minutes on low heat.

5. Remove the lid, add the brown onion paste and cook further till the lamb pieces are tender and the curry has thickened. Remove from heat and keep aside.

6. In a casserole or a baking dish, place alternate layers of rice and the lamb pieces. Sprinkle saffron and vetivier on top, cover with a wet cloth and cook on very low heat (dum) for 15-20 minutes.

7. Remove from heat, transfer to a serving dish and serve hot, garnished with golden fried onions and accompanied by Boondi raita (page 89). (Picture on page 85).

Prawn Biryani

Fresh prawns cooked with rice in delicate spices and vegetable stock

Serves: 4 , Preparation time: 1 hour, Cooking time: 25 minutes

Ingredients:

Prawns, shelled, deveined .... *100 gms*	Cloves *(laung)*... 4
Basmati rice ....*350 gms / 1 ³/₄ cup*	Bayleaves *(tej patta)* 4
Water... *400 ml / 2 cups*	Onions, sliced.. *40 gms / 2 ²/₃ tbs*
Salt to taste	Ginger-garlic paste *(page 13)* .... *10 gms / 2 tsp*
Turmeric powder *(haldi)* .... *a pinch*	Vegetable stock .... *750 litre / 3 ³/₄ cup*
Lemon .... ½	Salt .... *8 gms / 1 ²/₃ tsp*
Oil .... *15 ml / 1 tbs*	Butter .... *100 gms / ½ cup*
Cinnamon *(daalchini)* stick 1	Lemon 1/2
Green cardamom *(choti elaichi)* 4	Milk .... *50 ml / 3 ¹/₃ tbs*
Black cardamom *(bari elaichi)* 2	

Method:

1. Pick, wash and soak the rice for ½ hour. Drain and keep aside.

2. Take water in a pan, add salt to taste, turmeric powder and lemon juice. Bring to a boil and add the prawns. Cook till prawns are ³/₄ done. Remove, cut into small pieces, keep aside.

3. Heat oil in a handi *(pot)*. Add the whole spices, and sauté till they crackle, add the sliced onions and stir-fry to a golden brown. Add ginger-garlic paste dissolved in a little water.

4. Add the vegetable stock and bring to a boil. Add salt, butter (90 gms) and lemon juice.

5. Add the drained rice and cook on a medium heat, stirring occasionally.

6. When the water has reduced to the level of rice, sprinkle milk on top and cover with a wet cloth.

7. Put on very low heat (dum) for approx 15 minutes or till cooked. Remove from heat.

8. Heat the remaining butter and sauté the prawn pieces for a minute.

9. Transfer the rice to a serving dish and serve hot, garnished with prawns and accompanied by Bhindi raita, (page 87). (Picture on page 85).

Naan

A delicious Royal Indian Bread with a touch of onion and melon seeds

Serves: 4, Preparation time: 3 hours, Cooking time: 30 minutes

Ingredients:

Flour *(maida)* .... 1 kg	Yoghurt .... 150 gms / 3/4 cup
Salt .... 20 gms / 4 tsp	Water .... 400 ml / 2 cups
Baking powder .... 8 gms / 1 ½ tsp	Oil .... 20 ml / 4 tsp
Egg, whisked 2	Onion *(kalonji)* seeds .... 5 gms / 1 tsp
Sugar .... 30 gms / 2 tbs	Melon *(magaz)* seeds .... 5 gms / 1 tsp

Method:

1. Mix flour, salt, baking powder, egg, sugar and yoghurt. Add water to knead into a soft and smooth dough.
2. Add oil, knead and punch the dough, cover and keep aside to ferment for 2 hours.
3. Divide the dough into 8 balls, place on a lightly floured surface, sprinkle onion and melon seeds, flatten the balls slightly, cover and keep aside for 5 minutes.

4. Flatten each ball to make a round disc, stretch on one side to form an elongated oval.
5. Place carefully in a tandoor and cook till light brown spots occur on the surface.
6. Remove from the tandoor and serve hot, as an accompaniment to any curry dish. (Picture on page 84).

Tandoori Roti

Unleavened wheat flour pancakes cooked in a tandoor

Serves: 4, Preparation time: 1 hour 15 minutes, Cooking time: 20 minutes

Ingredients:

Whole wheat flour .... 1 kg	Water .... 700 ml / 3 ½ cups
Salt .... 20 gms / 4 tsp	

Method:

1. Seive flour and salt in a mixing bowl. Add water and knead into a smooth and elastic dough. Cover with a moist cloth and keep aside for 1 hour.
2. Place the dough on a floured board. Divide into 16 equal portions and shape into balls. Allow to rest for 5 minutes.

3. Flatten between palms moistened with a little water and oil.
4. Place carefully in a tandoor and cook till light brown in colour.
5. Remove from tandoor and serve, as an accompaniment to any curry dish. (Picture on page 84).

Stuffed Parantha

Spicy potato filling in a leavened whole wheat bread

Serves: 4, Preparation time: 30 minutes, Cooking time: 20 minutes

Ingredients:

Flour .... 200 gms / 1 cup	Green chillies, chopped .... 10 gms / 2 tsp
Butter .... 40 gms / 2 2/3 tbs	Green coriander, chopped .... 10 gms / 2 tsp
Water .... 80 ml / ½ cup	Salt .... 4 gms / 3/4 tsp
For the filling:	Red chilli powder .... 2 gms / 1/3 tsp
Potatoes, boiled, mashed .... 150 gms / 3/4 cup	Pomegranate *(anardana)* seeds .... 8 gms / 1½ tsp
Ginger, chopped .... 20 gms / 4 tsp	Oil .... 40 gms / 2 2/3 tbs

Method:

1. Mix butter into the flour and knead the flour using water into a smooth pliable dough.
2. For the filling, mix together the potatoes, ginger, green chillies, green coriander, salt, red chilli powder and pomegranate seeds. Divide the filling into 4 equal portions.
3. Divide the dough into 4 equal portions and shape into balls. Flatten each ball between palm and fingers. Place one portion of filling in the centre and seal the edges.

4. Dust with flour and roll out with a rolling pin into a 8" diameter pancake.
5. Heat a tawa *(griddle)*, brush the surface with oil. Place the stuffed parantha on the griddle and cook for a few seconds, brush with oil, turn over and similarly cook on the other side.
6. Both sides of the stuffed parantha should be crisp and delicately browned. Remove and serve immediately, accompanied by any yoghurt preparation.

Index